Florian Dombois, Julie Harboe (eds.)

Too Big To Scale – On Scaling Space, Numbers, Time and Energy

I0812048

Imprint

Editors: Florian Dombois, Julie Harboe
Graphic Design: Viola Zimmermann with Murielle Drack
Translation project management: Sebastian Viebahn
English-language editing: Burke Barrett and Margaret Hiley
Lithography and printing: Druckerei Odermatt AG, Dallenwil, Switzerland
Binding: Bubu AG, Mönchaltorf, Switzerland
Cover photo (8 May 2015): Brigham Baker

© 2017 Florian Dombois, Julie Harboe and Scheidegger & Spiess AG, Zurich
© for the texts: the authors
© for the images: see image credits

Despite best efforts, we have not been able to identify the holders of copyright and printing rights for all the illustrations. Copyright holders not mentioned in the credits are asked to substantiate their claims, and recompense will be made according to standard practice.

Verlag Scheidegger & Spiess AG
Niederdorfstrasse 54
8001 Zurich
Switzerland
www.scheidegger-spiess.ch

All rights reserved; no part of this work may be reproduced or edited using electronic systems, copied, or distributed in any form whatsoever without previous written consent from the publisher.

ISBN 978-3-85881-793-8

Content

Introduction

The People's Republic of China and Switzerland have had a Free Trade Agreement since 2014. Eight million people live in Switzerland, more than a billion in China – can concepts, modes of production, and methods be transferred from one country to the other? Since 1890, Levi's has produced a pair of trousers called *501* – is it still the same pair of pants today? Natural radiation exposure amounts to 0.3 mSv on average, and radioactive radiation of 7,000–10,000 mSv is fatal – what does the maximum legal value of 1 mSv mean for people in individual cases?

As diverse as these examples are, and despite the number of areas involved, there is a common theme: scaling. Scaling is a technique of changing size that has been used by people from time immemorial. Even as children, we begin to explore scale when playing, for example, with dolls, toy cars, and building blocks. And even in the oldest artistic artifacts such as the *Venus of Hohle Fels* or the *Chauvet* cave paintings, dating back to the beginnings of human history, the idea of representation and the notion of scalability seem to be twinned.

In the course of industrialization in the nineteenth and twentieth centuries, this anthropological technique of scaling took another surprising turn. First, the art of engineering developed so dramatically that ever-higher towers and ever-longer bridges were built, for which small models were enlarged cleverly and thus scaled. The work of Gustave Eiffel, for instance, would be inconceivable without free thinking in different scales.

In addition, because of mass production scaling achieved a further incredible reality. Things that are developed in one place subsequently assume a global existence. Today, we live in a world that is dominated by scaled objects. Unique pieces have become special cases among our household goods, our clothing, our public spaces. Actually, is there any object at all in our surroundings that does *not* have scaled relatives or that was *not*, at least hypothetically, conceived originally in a different dimension? And haven't we even gone so far as to introduce scaling in our gestures since 2007, when we started enlarging and reducing photographs with thumb and forefinger on our smartphones to adapt the size of pictures?

This book and the conference preceding it were the result of a further observation: The omnipresence of scaled objects in our surroundings has been accompanied by photography for nearly 200 years. And it is our assumption that photographic and film cameras have not only documented the growing importance of scaling in the modern age, but have contributed essentially to making many intellectual pursuits possible to begin with. For every camera lens scales its object on a negative (or a digital 'back wall') and subsequently repeats the *scaling of size* the moment the image is reproduced on the proof or the screen. In a photo camera, the Eiffel Tower can be exposed on a negative to be the same size as a fruit fly.

We do not only seek to relate scaling to space, however – as a second dimension, we want to have a look at the *scaling of time*, of its acceleration and deceleration, which manifests itself in film particularly in the form of slow motion and fast forward. Using this technique, new things and processes in reality become visible, and thus their manipulation – we believe – becomes conceivable in the first place. In other words, perceptual and intellectual spaces interlock in technical images of reality; photographic reproduction is not only a model *of* the world, but also a model *for* the world. What is seen gives rise to a new way of seeing.

Third, we would like to discuss *scaling of film speed (energy)* as a hypothesis and a theme. Regarding photographic and film cameras, film speed (the sensitivity to light) would be of interest insofar as it is adapted to the exposure to light – and thus a form of energy – for example in the cinematographic "day for night" method, which allows a set filmed during the daytime to be used to represent a night environment;

or conversely, filming is done with infrared material, turning darkness into daylight.

And fourth, *scaling of number* is found in photography in the reproduction of prints and the displays, on which photos appear everywhere nowadays. Parallel to the much-evoked flood of images, today there is a flood-like repetition of the same images over and over again. We live in a world of many different images, but also of many of the same images.

Digitalization takes much of this to the extreme. At the software level, there are no scales; all of the representations of objects are made without dimensions. The world inside the computer has no scale units; virtual objects take on a specific size only in conjunction with the world outside of the computer – by means of a display, a beamer, a printer. Like the photo camera, the computer can also put large and small objects indifferently next to each other; temporal processes can be recorded at a faster speed or stretched out; and weak differences can be enhanced or vice versa. Also the scaling of number implies a fundamental change when applied within the digital realm; while we used to be able to differentiate between original and copy, model and reproduction, negative and proof, in digital objects theoretically no differences can be seen any more.

Publication

This publication is devoted to the phenomenon of scaling from different perspectives and attempts to show that it is omnipresent. We are concerned with different perceptions of scaling, different ways in which scaling is made visible, and different ways in which it can be explored. And in several places we compare scaling with camera reality.

To this end, we organized a symposium on May 8–9, 2015, bringing the contributors together in the form of a *'Palaver'*. The *'Palaver'* is a spatial arrangement developed by Florian Dombois and Eran Schaerf in 2008 to negotiate individual artworks (see Dombois and Schaerf 2008). For this purpose, the room is divided by a screen and on both sides a camera records what is happening and transmits it live to a monitor on the other side. In the meantime, this spatial arrangement has proven suitable for conference formats in which science and humanities lectures encounter artistic interventions and performances, putting discursive and performative action at the same level and thus neither giving the academics an advantage over the artists, nor vice versa (see e.g. Dombois et al. 2014). Showing and telling are put on an equal footing. In our thematic field, the *'Palaver'* format took on special significance because each contribution and each discussion could always be seen on the monitor, thus allowing attendants to witness them in a scaled filmic reality.

In this book, the question of how to negotiate the contributions is posed anew. For while some essays may take more similar stances than others, and although the contributors learned from each other thanks to the two days they spent together in May 2015, not just one but many lines of argumentation can be developed. Hence the following sequence is just one of many possible ones.

In the first contribution, *Andrew Fisher* supports the thesis of the conference delineated above that the camera is a major protagonist connecting a technical and epistemic understanding of scale. We see that there is more to this mix than the scaling of magnitude or the unending option of reproductions. Fisher invites us to surf on the giant wave of images which the camera has produced and suggests that we gain balance by activating our capability for imaginative variations. Thinking about scale and the photographic thus enables us to grasp some of photography's irreducible elements and introduces us to the idea of scale per se as a means of creating specific horizons.

Sarine Waltenspül shows how the relationship between the model, which holds the key to explaining scale in film, and its partner, the camera, take on different roles and how both are used for playing games with forms of representation. To what extent is it part of the story that the translation of scale is made explicitly visible in film? Does the presence of the model as a deliberate construction denote a mature film audience? What are the deeper implications of such aesthetics of scaling?

The Japanese researcher Masanao Abe set up his photographic equipment and for more than 15 years photographed and traced the movements of clouds around the iconic Mount Fuji. *Helmut Völter* describes how Abe tried to understand the physical changes through the images. Today we can hardly grasp the scientific scale of the project; all we are left with is an outsized heritage of the passing clouds.

Offering both a historical and a disciplinary perspective is key to *Reinhard Wendler's* introduction to scaling. Expanding from architecture into other scientific fields Wendler shows that the complexity of scaling demands a focus on the specificity of problems. Still, scaling effects and their phenomena today present options for a multidisciplinary and well-founded encounter with the topic.

In her contribution, *Juliet Koss* examines the significance of scaling and models in the young Soviet republic during the first two decades after the October Revolution. For her piece, she chooses the format of a book proposal, which can be seen as the model for a book that still has to be written. This approach corresponds exactly to that of the Soviet artists she examined, who via models and photographs envisioned a not-yet-built future for their country.

In fiction, anything goes, and *Mirjam Steiner* shows in her contribution how literature is a scale-free space. With no material constraints, only the authors' ability to regulate the readers' imagination sets the limits. Authors such as Jonathan Swift, Lewis Carroll and Friedrich Dürrenmatt have all practiced the art of writing in(to) fantastic dimensions.

From very different points of view, *Julie Harboe* and the joint authors *Simon Grand and Christoph*

Weckerle argue that human activity and creativity play an important role in relation to scale.

Grand and Weckerle approach the cultural and creative industries (CCI) as a large-scale political concept defining an area of high potential for innovation and financial development. They compare this large-scale view with the small-scale approach of individual creative professionals and see curating as a constructive way of combining very different 'force fields'.

Man as the measure of all things has been gradually excluded from scientific measurements, yet the history of science shows how the role of the people doing science, from Ludwik Fleck's observation of bacteriological experiments to the IPCC, represents the essential core of the production of scientific knowledge. So what are the benchmarks for scientific collaborations and can we reintroduce respect for the human scale and intuition into scientific reasoning? In a metaphorical act of reverse engineering, Harboe scales four research groups in a wind tunnel and presents readers with layered models enabling an about face, where the viewer regains authority.

Looking at the scales involved in defining color, *Adrien Lucca* shows us how his art creates approximations that provide a means of understanding highly complex differentiations. The subject is so sensitive that here the sciences have resorted to using individual scale to tame randomness.

Frank Schweitzer introduces us to the issue of how science can take the initiative and resolutely formulate systemic properties to deal with scaling highly complex forms of data. The scientific definitions supported by equations and their algorithms take us into a space not unlike that of the architectural theorists. Alongside solid interpretations this development of scaling also involves new emerging properties challenging linearity and the scientist's control.

The board of McDonald's is responsible for 68 million meals a day being served globally. *Haseeb Ahmed* sees the possible collaboration with McDonald's and the Wind Tunnel World, which for the past 100 years has streamlined and tested objects. The vortex man found by Ahmed as an actor in the Wind Tunnel World unites the two approaches.

Olivier Chazot bases his work on the interfaces between concrete testing of aerodynamic flows in wind tunnels by the Von Karman Institute in Brussels and the translation into theory or abstracted definitions. In doing so, he builds a bridge that has to carry the weight of physical objects as well as that of the philosophical context.

To sum up, the order in which we offer the essays in this volume continually oscillates between overview and close up, between general theoretical work and delving into case study. Thematically, the contributions move from the environment of photography to the field of architecture, then turn to political visual language and literature, cast a glance at the economy and system research, and finally arrive at wind tunnel research, which apart from many other scalability issues presents so-called scale effects, which determine the size of the wind tunnel models and their significance, constituting both a concrete and symbolic representation of the scaling problem.

Size Matters

This book and the studies on scaling in it emerged in the context of our research project, 'Size Matters. On Scale and Size of Models', which was sponsored over a period of 42 months by the Swiss National Science Foundation from 2013 to 2016. Under the direction of Florian Dombois, Haseeb Ahmed, Julie Harboe (7/2014–12/2015), Sarine Waltenspül, and Reinhard Wendler (1/2013–6/2014) worked together in the narrower project team, and Martin Burr, Kaspar König, and Mirjam Steiner in the extended team. At the center of the research was our own artistic wind tunnel, which beyond aeronautic research served as a place of engagement between different disciplines, as well as a projection screen for the approaches and methods the contributors brought with them. In other words, the fundamental investigation of the issue of models and scaling is carried out in a very concrete environment that is not at all dimensionless, but claims a reality of real size within the Zurich University of the Arts. In such an investigation, the view invariably oscillates between the metaphorical and the symbolic significance of one's work and the respective specific articulation. Or as Hans-Jörg Rheinberger put it during his first visit (30 April 2013): "This wind tunnel is a model of a second order and at the same time unsettlingly specific." The topic of scaling and models is thus always also a method and self-perception, oscillating between the object of observation and the manner of observing.

The design of this book, too, follows this oscillating approach: each essay is printed on a separate sheet. Thus each author is given an equal amount of space. Each essay has 16 pages to spread out, resulting in large type sizes in the case of short texts, and small type sizes in the case of long texts. Theoretically, if you cut up the inner block of this book, separating the individual layers again, you would get the 13 contributions neatly divided and marked by the black-and-white rulers in the book's fold. These rulers measure the line spacing of each essay. Put another way, here bookbinding means actually physically linking all the contributions. We do what we mean.

Acknowledgements

We would like to thank all of the authors for their contributions, for the good discussions and the cross-disciplinary exchange. Such a divergent coming together of different worldviews and methods requires a willingness to translate knowledge across different disciplines as well as the ability to question things fundamentally.

In addition, we would like to thank the Swiss National Science Foundation for the generous three-year financing of the project, which is all the more noteworthy since we did not approach the subject of scaling and models based on a work plan with predefined work packages, but on a method of work we call *Fahrkunst*. Using this method, which is quite unusual for the sciences insofar as it is not the objective that is defined in advance, but rather the rhythms and forces that drive the research, was essential to give the artistic work sufficient room.

Finally, we extend thanks to the Zurich University of the Arts for their wholehearted support, enabling us to carry out our work. For although the Swiss National Science Foundation provides substantial funding for third-party-funding projects, including our own, its sponsorship of our project was not sufficient to finance all of the activities, publications, and the construction of the wind tunnel. The project would not have been possible without the university's generous support.

English translation by Burke Barrett

References

Dombois, Florian, and Eran Schaerf, 2008, *Palaver*. Bern/Berlin.

Dombois, Florian, Mira Fliescher, Dieter Mersch and Julia Rintz (eds.), 2014, *Ästhetisches Denken. Nicht-Propositionalität, Episteme, Kunst*. Zurich: Diaphanes.

Florian Dombois (*1966, Berlin) is an artist who has focused on time, models, landforms, labilities, wind and tectonic activity. He has been a professor at Zurich University of the Arts, Switzerland since 2011. In 2010, he received the German Sound Art Prize.

Julie Harboe is an art historian, critic and curator. Among other tasks she co-founded and managed an art space, developed and coordinated a unit for artistic research and is currently a lecturer at Future Laboratory CreaLab and Lucerne School of Business. She focuses on transdisciplinary collaborations in research, education, business and art.

Andrew Fisher

Imaginative Variation: Photographic Scale and Photographic Horizons

Andrew Fisher

Imaginative Variation: Photographic Scale and Photographic Horizons

> *[T]here is no single site of the photograph. [...] There is a distributive unity to the photograph itself.*
>
> Peter Osborne, *Anywhere or Not at All*

A reordering and re-envisioning of the photographic

This essay sets out to explore three terms that are important to photography, namely scale, horizon and imaginative variation. The relationships between these will be explored with an emphasis on questions of scale, not only because it is the least familiar in the photographic context, but also because it links and gives shape to what the others might mean for photography.

We use photography to establish horizons of meaning that might help to orient us visually within a complex world. But its promise to perform this function, to render the world proportionate, is often duplicitous. One might go as far to say that precisely insofar as it holds out such imaginative possibilities, photography also serves as an agent of disorientation and disproportion. In general, the term photography might be thought of as naming the set of horizons thus promised and the processes through which they are created, used, contested and dissolved. In this light, photography appears as a massively determined and complex form of social imagination: a complex process of imaginative variation on the world.

Since its inception, photography has come to inform and to transform the spatial and temporal, epistemological and phenomenological horizons of experience associated with almost all spheres of life, and has done so in many and various ways. It has long since served, for instance, as an important vehicle of practical and imaginative possibilities taken up by individuals. And it endures as a major instrument through which the prospects offered by political, cultural and economic institutions are given shape. One can link these functions of photography to recent critical debates and ask whether, perhaps, we have 'lost' the horizons of meaning and value that might have oriented us in the past and now need to turn to image forms that could help us construct new horizons. Or, alternatively, one might ask whether the expectation that new social forms might constitute themselves through the image's projection of novel horizons is fatefully circumscribed by a broader and overdetermining "horizon of endless accumulation [...] politically coded in economic terms as the freedom of ever greater consumption", as Peter Osborne (2011: 127) has it.

This essay adopts a metacritical approach to these questions and possibilities. It sets out to think of photography as a form that promises and withholds, constitutes and dissolves the very possibility of establishing horizons of meaning and value. Hence, the essay's remit is to work towards understanding the relationship between the imagination (figured as a technology of imaginative variation) and the horizons of meaning and value associated with it (through a kind of diastolic/systolic rhythm of promise and dissolution). In photography, I argue, a key mechanism of these operations and relations is scale.

One might take a step to one side here and note that issues of scale are integral to photography and have been since its earliest days. Though much writing on photography and many different spheres of photographic practice entail significant questions and facts of scale, surprisingly little sustained and explicit critical or theoretical attention has been paid to this fact.

In response, this essay sets out to explore the senses of scale encountered in, disclosed by and established through the photographic. In fact, it sets out to reorient the way in which photography is understood according to these relationships. Scale and horizon are explored here as closely related and vital aspects of the photographic and as two facets of a matrix of processes and possibilities that shape what photography might mean and what it might do in the present, that is, the horizons of meaning it both proffers and serves to destruct and the form photography takes as an imaginative variation on the world.

Photographic operations of and at scale and the manner in which these might hold out or threaten to dissolve horizons of photographic meaning and value appear ever more obvious in, and indeed vital to, the contemporary context. On the one hand, photography continues to hold out the historically familiar promise that it might enable some kind of meaningful orientation within and towards a complex and disorientating world. (For a discussion of related issues in which the terms horizon and orientation are central, see Ahmed 2006). On the other hand, the contemporary form of the photographic – its computational and networked character and the uses this enables – undermines the possibility of establishing and maintaining meaningful horizons of experience. Photography continues to promise that the world might be set to measure and that events unfolding within it might be rendered proportionate. (For a resonant discussion of proportionality and disproportionality as they shape our political present, see Weizman 2012: 1–27.) In the very act of providing them, it seems, the photographic also produces conditions of disorientation and literal experiences of de-rangement that threaten to dissolve what might give epistemological and phenomenological horizons coherence, stability and efficacy. These issues and this terminology shape a range of recent writings on the contemporary image, from the vertiginous dissolution of pictorial perspective and the horizons it may once have offered in Hito Steyerl's writings on networked digital culture (Steyerl 2012) to the *Former West* curatorial project and its critical concern for contemporary horizons of social expectation and political possibility (for contrasting views on these questions, see the contributions to this project by Sheikh 2011 and Osborne 2011). In relation to scale and by way of further contextualization, one might also remark Timothy Clark's account of the derangements of scale associated with impending environmental disaster and the gap between individual agency and global processes this entails (Clark 2009). And finally, one might link these questions to the generalized techno-scientific crisis of "disorientation as such" diagnosed by Bernard Stiegler in his *Technics and Time* (Stiegler 2009: 3).

However, the question remains: why would all of this encourage one to think or try to rethink photography in terms of scale? And, for that matter, what senses are the terms *scale* and *photography* being given here? A convincing answer to these questions, I argue, only emerges when one takes seriously the marked variation in meaning that these terms take on in relation to one another.

The quotation from Peter Osborne used as an epigram above might give a clue to what is at stake here. In the face of its recent technical-historical transformation, Osborne characterises the contemporary photograph – an object whose antecedents are often fetishized as the basic 'unit' of photography – as a distributed unity. The photograph's conventionally statically conceived and objectively bounded unity is now dispersed, pluralized and rendered processual. Its material existence as an image-object is no longer guaranteed by the limit of a singular and discrete object, if ever it was. Whilst the photograph nonetheless persists as a familiar site around which social investments, cultural identifications, means of knowing and modes of sensible association might cohere, the conditions that underpin these possibilities are radically altered and destabilized. This viewpoint considerably complicates the material forms and modes of space and time commonly associated with the photograph and, by implication, throws into question how these inform the experiences, uses and meanings that a photograph could be expected to enable.

The notion of the photograph as a distributive unity would seem to place great emphasis on what can count as a whole or as a part in this set of photographic relations. Because of this, whilst Osborne's problematization of the photograph as a unitary object rings true, one might still be left asking (at risk of being reductive) exactly what parts of the photograph, what features of the photographic apparatus and what specific functions of their material distribution are complicated, displaced and set in motion.

What is projected here is a situation characterized by a fundamental reordering and re-envisioning of relationships between, on the one hand, the operations and functions inherent to photographic images and apparatuses and, on the other hand, the horizons of meaning, use and value that these might be expected to establish and sustain. One might begin to make sense of the photograph as a distributive unity by noting that, as a conceptual figure, distributed unity foregrounds the relationship between dispersed material and technical moments of the photograph whilst also articulating the scope and reach of its possible uses. Considering the photograph as a generalized site of distributive unity raises questions concerning the intertwined material, cultural, technical and geopolitical horizons that photographs and their uses, meanings and imaginative possibilities might entail, project and operate within. Starting out from an analysis of variations in the meaning of scale in the photographic context enables one to elucidate the workings of such horizons and the importance of this for an understanding of the contemporary situation of photography. This also entails beginning at least to rethink what the photographic is as a form of imagination.

Scale and the photographic

So, what does the term *scale* already mean in and for photography?[1] Many already specified notions of scale are familiar in this context, though they remain under-examined as such. Notable amongst these is the often remarked fact that photographic images achieve their strong reality effects whilst radically de- and rescaling what they depict (see, for instance, Kracauer 1960: 4–5, Benjamin 1972: 202–203, Barthes 1981: 12–13, Sontag 1979: 4, Därmann 1995: 268–274, Wells 2013: 119–160). The techniques through which these sliding scales of actualization operate also open up photographs to other kinds of scaled variation, like the changing modes of reproduction inscribing them in large-scale processes of mass production, dissemination and consumption. Remarking on this is another staple gesture of writing about photography (see Benjamin 1969: 217–252, Busch 1989: 126–154, Flusser 2000: 65–75 and 2013: 75–82, Virilio 1994, Nancy 2005: 106–107). Moreover, the fact that photographs are taken to be representations in the first place derives from variable and associated technical processes organized into an apparatus that is oriented to set the appearance of things in scaled relation to one another, such as through the camera control of focus, exposure and aperture (cf. Flusser 2013: 195–201). Spatial and temporal relationships between things are registered through a predetermined combination of scaling operations that offers and circumscribes a range of possibilities according to which orders and ratios of scale – for instance, relative size and position, surface area and overlap, acuity and blur – are established in the making of a photographic image. These explicit scaling operations condition photographic images and afford their representational effects (Maynard 2008: 187–209). They are also, however, determined *as* conditions by the various bodies of technical knowledge and commercial interest governing the industries that produce photographic apparatuses and the technologized image cultures these facilitate and seek to exploit (cf. Flusser 2000, Osborne 2013: 117–131, Stiegler 2009: 118–122, Cunningham 2012).

1 The projection of scale as an issue for photography in this section draws closely on my discussions of this theme elsewhere (see Fisher 2013 and 2016).

One can note, even on the basis of these brief observations, that the photographic context is saturated with conceptually and practically differentiated concerns for scale and that these different 'scales' are nonetheless interconnected. On these bases, one might say that the photograph is marked by what one might call interior and exterior horizons, vectors of scaled relation, so to speak, that characterize what the photographic image is, what it might do, and how it might do so. And the interplay between these horizons is made emphatic when one thinks of the photograph as a distributed unity. The interior horizon of a photographic image is inherently scaled according to a concrete assemblage of technical scaling operations and material conditions of phenomenological encounter, which also open the photograph onto what one might correspondingly call exterior horizons of social and economic processes with different but also explicitly scaled characteristics. These different senses of scale and processes of scaling meet each other in the photograph. Indeed, one might say that, *qua* images, photographs exist in, or perhaps better *as*, the tension between intercalated and simultaneously operative horizons of scale, scaling and scalability. The contrast between such *interior* and *exterior* horizons is labile and not bounded by any single instantiation of the photograph as an object.

There are other important senses of scale to note here, however. One might start out again on a different tack by remarking upon other, more explicit and strictly delimited conceptions of scale that already inform particular photographic practices, such as specialized techniques of photogrammetry and the broader possibilities of photomensuration (the use of photography to measure things). Here, the notion of scale can take on highly specified meanings that are ultimately reducible to relative numerical values, the uses of which can never quite disentangle themselves from the interests that govern their founding claims to abstraction (cf. Arendt 2007, Kelsey 2011: 10–16, Sekula 1986: 3–64, Farocki 2004: 193–202, Daston and Galison 2010: 115–190, Elkins 2011: 98–158). But even when highly specialized – as often hard-won and useful protocols for setting things to reliable scales of measure and relative proportion – such uses of photography remain refinements and extensions of a generic propensity that is common to all photographic apparatuses and is implied by all photographic images, albeit to a more or less obvious extent. Photography entails the setting of a certain perspective on things into a calculable form – an image derived from a technical apparatus – out of which might be extrapolated a more or less exact practice of recalculation that is oriented towards establishing the measure of something (Flusser 2013: 91–98, Fisher 2016). Practices and protocols of photomensuration thus stand as second-order modes of abstraction and calculation that rest on strategies for disambiguating photography's propensity for setting things to scale. That various modes of specialized measurement (explicit modes of scaling) can be achieved by using photographic means derives as a possibility from those modes of scale, scaling and scalability that are harboured in the photographic as such.Attention to specific practices of scaling that use photography foregrounds the ways in which they exploit this fundamental characteristic of photography. Starting out from the delimited technical senses that the term scale has already accrued in photographic practice leads one back to a more general and ambiguous sense of the scalar character of the photographic as such. (Maurice Merleau-Ponty's 'working note' of 1960 on the ontological significance of the notion of scale in *The Visible and the Invisible* provides a very suggestive guide to thinking about this. See Merleau-Ponty 1968: 226–227.)

Together, these different starting points – and the ways in which they complicate the meaning of scale in the photographic context – combine to suggest a further response to the problems projected and questions asked at the outset. An intuition guides the answer: that consideration paid to the status of variations on the meaning of scale and the relationships pertaining between these actually matters very much to our understanding of the photographic. And a way of articulating where this might lead has already been implied. The diverse, discrete and concrete levels at which the term scale already applies to photography suggest that they are interlinked and ultimately codependent. This indicates, I argue, that a variegated operation of differing but coincident senses of scale, modes of scaling, scaled phenomena and conditions of scalability is a constant in and for the photographic. The variation in and, crucially, the *play* between these photographic senses of scale – and not any one particular fact, phenomenon, technique, order or discourse of scale alone – is what needs to be imagined and held in view in order that it might be conceptualized and evaluated. (For a parallel conception of scale articulated in terms of historiography, see Ricoeur 2004: 209–216.) How might one approach this task?

Imaginative variation: discovering the principle of a variation in photographic scales

This essay is encouraging you to entertain the notion that an inherently variegated combination of senses, operations and phenomena of scale is a ubiquitous and necessary feature of *all* photographies and that this fact is significant. In support of these claims I would like to propose a thought experiment.

Try, for a moment, to think about photography without referring to the easily accepted authority of the idea that it is, at root, a medium of representational images; without privileging one or other favoured artistic, personal or scientific use of photographs; and without taking for granted familiar critical tropes such as photography's widespread institutionalization as a vehicle of identification and encounter with others.

Suspend your interest in all of this for a while and, bearing in mind its multifaceted and hybrid character, allow your imagination to zoom in and out whilst ranging as freely as possible over different aspects of the photographic, including *anything* that might suggest itself as a variation on it. If, in doing this, what occurs to you retains a sense of belonging under the heading of the photographic, dwell on it for a while to see what, if anything, is distinctive about this. The photographic will no doubt prove an expansive, multilayered and capricious category and if you approach this task honestly the horizons of its imaginative variation will appear effectively infinite. The promiscuity with which unexpected connections between otherwise distinct aspects of photography might arise will make the object of your reflection bewildering in its complexity. But don't short-circuit the experiment because of this. For now, you are just being asked to put to one side any determinate concern for customary ways of understanding and experiencing photography so as to consider what might emerge in their place, allowing other connections to suggest themselves and keeping an eye on how one thing leads to another in the process so that, later on, you can evaluate the significance of what occurred to you, recall what seemed to link these things together and assess whether this emergent connectedness might turn out to be important.

Some readers will no doubt recognize that this thought experiment draws on aspects of Edmund Husserl's methodological procedure of "phenomenological reduction". In fact, the experiment isolates one key conceptual strategy of this reduction, namely, "imaginative variation" (Husserl 1983: 131–141; see also Renaud Barbaras's critical refiguration of the Husserlian reduction, Barbaras 2006: 44–80). But, having noted this connection – perhaps also whilst flagging up the eccentric focus, scope and orientation it is given here – further consideration of this reference to Husserl can be set to one side, at least for the purposes of this essay, as it is the operation of the strategy of imaginative variation and the implications of this operation that are of direct concern here (see Fisher 2009). The thought experiment you have just been encouraged to take part in adumbrates the form taken by photography insofar as it operates as an imaginative variation on the world.

At risk of stating the obvious, a first thing to note is that, depending on who performs it and from which starting point, this reflective procedure will always produce different articulations of the photographic. Insofar as it presupposes an open community of performers, of necessity, this strategy traces multiple pathways through the territory of the photographic and the vast range of things upon which it touches. Nevertheless, I argue, that in their very difference, these multiple possible trajectories share a characteristic: they bind together diverse aspects of the photographic as possibilities and do so in a process that is effectively unending. And this helps in attempting to conceptualize the hybrid, changeable and complex character of the photographic.

This exercise of imaginative variation exceeds its initial function as a heuristic device that encourages one to reflect anew on the photographic. The effectively infinite and differentiated horizon of imaginative variability that emerges through this is, I argue, actually an important general characteristic of the photographic. The effectively infinite extension and the necessarily plural and differentiated status of its imaginative variations establishes an interesting relation to the massively determined and highly complex horizon of words and things, processes and forms that stand as diverse but integral aspects of the photographic. And this enables one to conceive of the photographic in its complex outlines as a realm of imaginative possibilities. However difficult the photographic might be to encompass in thought or to grasp practically, one only ever encounters or is able to conceive of it through particular instances, objects, practices, conventions and forms such as those outlined above (including those that were put to one side at the outset of the thought experiment). The methodological strategy of imaginative variation suggests a way of holding in view a sense of photography as itself a kind of imaginative variation. But what does this mean and what has it to do with the analysis of photography and scale?

Another important feature to emerge from this process of willed, free-ranging and imaginative variation is the importance of scale for photography. Abstracting from the conventionalized attitudes according to which photographs are often thought reveals that some admixture of various photographic senses of scale is always present, whichever pathway through the photographic may be taken. Start out on the experiment again. This time limit yourself to imaginatively varying the ways in which a range of different and modulating senses of scale – some of which were sketched above – feature in whatever aspect, form or moment of photography that comes into consideration. Though the senses of scale, scaling and scalability that emerge will obviously differ, some combination of scalar factors will always be identifiable. Out of this process an expanded notion of the photographic meaning of scale emerges as nothing less than one of photography's irreducible elements.

Because of the wide variation in its photographic senses, scale is an intuitable feature of all the possible photographies that might be imagined in this way. The conceptual gambit pursued in this essay is to take this imaginatively emergent ubiquity a step further. Without having to add anything to the connections that emerge in this way, one can conceptually generalize the persistent occurrence of such meanings and operations of scale as a necessary feature, namely, as the principle of a variation in the scales of the photographic and the significance of the play between these.

This principle can be given an adjectively inflected noun form. It is an *ineluctable variegation* – an unavoidable characteristic of diversification – that gives overall shape to the meaning of scale in the context of photography and that takes the form of a semantic and praxial 'unity in diversification' of the many senses and uses of scale harboured within the photographic. Arrays of photographic equipment, the photographic images that result from them and the practices out of which these emerge, coalesce as orchestrations of different modalities of scale. Though always contingent, some such variegated orchestration of scales is also always at work in all possible photographies. To make, to use, to mediate and to encounter a photographic image is to be inscribed within a play between variegated phenomena, operations and facts of scale.

This expanded and variable notion of scale, I argue, describes the concrete form photography takes on in its function as a massively determined imaginative variation of the world. As such, it also suggests itself as a key mechanism through which horizons of meaning and value might be instituted or destabilized and how these processes might be critically thought.

Photographic Horizons

One might start out again on yet another tack by asking what the term horizon means in and for photography. The answers parallel the operations of scale and the form of imaginative variation articulated above. Amongst its many possible meanings for photography, horizon most obviously denotes the division of pictorial space that promises a perspective on what might be depicted in a photograph. Such pictorial organization entails the preparation of frames for perceptual attention so that one might become absorbed in an image or set it to one side in favour of something else. And this foregrounds the phenomenological sense of horizon as a process in which an object of attention stands out against its surrounding environment and in which one's concern for the former sets the concerns of the latter in abeyance for a time. In a vernacular vein, photographs serve conventionally to orient the production of social meaning and to provide nodal points around which a range of personal values and experiences might cohere (Ahmed 2006: 89–90). As Ahmed remarks, far from being neutral and unmotivated, such horizons take shape according to dominant expectations informing what orientations might be affirmed, for instance, as they are inscribed with sexed, gendered and raced values. The orienting function of horizons acts normatively to affirm or to denigrate those who find themselves positioned within them. In the photographic context, the meaning of the term horizon cannot be constrained by pictorial concerns or by the valorization of immediate experience, though it structures the former and gives tenor to the latter. Here, what is on the verge of the discrete photographic image acts as an unstable horizon. What is going on at these verges, one should note, is swept up into the tension between the photograph as a discrete site of concern and its status as a distributed unity. Photographically, experiences are spatialized and temporalized in complex and disjunctive ways, establishing what one might call interruptive horizons that layer the immediate physical environment with distant things and past events, that collocate experience of the here and now with otherwise invisible, antecedent or anticipated phenomena, and that do so in ways that exceed purely visual processes. Thus, the term horizon suggests a machinic parallel to the situated limits of human vision as well as, crucially, signifying a range of prosthetic photographic capacities that promise to overcome these limits. The phenomenological senses of horizon, then, appear to be interlaced through photography with other technical and historical, temporal and spatial, social and political senses that the term also assumes. It likewise refers one to those modes of bodily and machinic comportment entailed in acts of photographing and being photographed and it sets *these* horizons in the expansive scope and reach of the photographic as a suite of cultural and historical processes.

This brief rehearsal of some possible photographic meanings of the term horizon parallels the description of photography's ineluctably variegated scales made earlier in the essay. The analogy between them is by no means accidental or merely rhetorical. The photographic senses of horizon are inherently scaled. The scaled character of the photographic is tied up with its articulation of horizons.

Returning to and expanding upon a point made earlier might help in making sense of what connects these layered determinations of the term horizon to the notion of scale developed above. A basic function of photographic apparatuses is to register the ostensible spatial and temporal state of things, to fix these together at certain scales of relation and according to a combination of prefigured operations of scale and anticipations of scaled outcomes. One implication of thinking about the photographic in this way is that one never encounters 'space' or 'time' – nor, for that matter, any place, thing, moment or event – other than through a combination of processes that entail the possibility of setting salient aspects of appearance to scale in the more or less enduring but also changeable form of an image. If *to scale* in this sense is a basic function of photography – the interior horizon of the photograph as image – photographs and photographic apparatuses of all kinds are also, as a matter of principle, subject to the demands of what I earlier called exterior horizons that entail their *being scaled, de-* and *re-scaled*, thus making scalability a fundamental feature of the photographic.

Whilst the relationship between such interior and exterior horizons may appear relatively fixed from any one vantage point, they are never entirely static, nor are they ever totally distinct. One might think of them as vectors of scaled and scaling relation, as operations that fill out what 'distribution' might mean as a condition of the contemporary photograph and as a way of thinking these technical or apparatic conditions as intimately intertwined with broader processes. In this vein, for instance, one can note that photographically mediated desires and the photographic potential for setting things to measure or proportion, useful bodies of photographic knowledge and moments of affective immediacy in the face of photographs all share the characteristic of arising out of and being enabled by a play between scaled relations that set the terms for any horizon of possibility, meaning and value they may promise.

By way of a brief conclusion, one can remark that questions asked about the meaning of scale in and for photography are, it turns out, questions asked about the horizons held out by photographs, the promises these entail and also often disappoint. Articulation of these relationships fills out the distributive unity of the contemporary photograph and renders it thinkable as a play between scales; a series of modulations in the ineluctable variegation of scale that cast and recast themselves in and as our photographic horizons. It is in this sense that scale and horizon promise to help one understand the problematic of photography as a form of imaginative variation on the world.

References

Ahmed, Sara, 2006, *Queer Phenomenology: Orientations, Objects, Others.* Durham and London: Duke University Press.

Arendt, Hannah, 2007, 'The Conquest of Space and the Stature of Man' in *The New Atlantis* 18 (Fall): 43–55.

Barbaras, Renaud, 2006, *Desire and Distance: Introduction to a Phenomenology of Perception* (trans. Paul B. Milan). Stanford, CA: Stanford University Press.

Barthes, Roland, 1981, *Camera Lucida: Reflections on Photography* (trans. Richard Howard). New York: Hill and Wang.

Benjamin, Walter, 1969, 'The Work of Art in the Age of Mechanical Reproduction' (trans. Harry Zohn) in Arendt, Hannah (ed.), *Illuminations.* New York: Schocken Books: 217–252.

Benjamin, Walter, 1972, 'A Short History of Photography' (trans. William Ivins Jr.) in Trachtenberg, Alan (ed.), *Classic Essays on Photography.* New Haven, Connecticut: Leete's Island Books: 199–216.

Busch, Bernd, 1989, *Belichtete Welt: Eine Wahrnehmungsgeschichte der Fotografie.* München: Carl Hanser Verlag.

Clark, Timothy, 2012, 'Derangements of Scale' in Cohen, Tom (ed.), *Telemorphosis: Theory in the Era of Climate Change vol. 1.* Ann Arbor: Open Humanities Press, University of Michigan Library: 148–166.

Cohnen, Thomas, 2008, *Fotografischer Kosmos: Der Beitrag eines Mediums zur visuellen Ordnung der Welt.* Bielefeld: Transcript Verlag.

Cunningham, Nathanial, 2012, *Face Value: An Essay on the Politics of Photography.* New York: Working Group.

Daston, Lorraine, and Peter Galison, 2010, *Objectivity.* New York: Zone Books.

Därmann, Iris, 1995, *Tod und Bild: Eine phänomenologische Mediengeschichte.* Munich: Wilhelm Fink Verlag.

Elkins, James, 2008, *Six Stories from the End of Representation: Images in Painting, Photography, Astronomy, Microscopy, Physics and Quantum Mechanics, 1980–2000.* Stanford, CA: Stanford University Press.

Elkins, James, 2011, *What Photography Is.* London and New York: Routledge.

Fisher, Andrew, 2009, 'Beyond Barthes: Rethinking the Phenomenology of Photography' in *Radical Philosophy 157* (Sept./Oct.): 19–29.

Fisher, Andrew, 2013, 'Photographic Scale' in *On the Verge of Photography: Imaging beyond Representation.* Birmingham: ARTicle Press: 151–170.

Fisher, Andrew, 2014, 'Photo-Surveillance and the Emplaced Déraciné' in *Photographies* 7(1): 53–66.

Fisher, Andrew, 2016, 'On the Scales of Photographic Abstraction' in *Photographies* 9(2): 203–215.

Flusser, Vilém, 2012, 'Towards a Theory of Techno-Imagination' (trans. Anna Wojtachno) in *Philosophy of Photography* 2(2): 195–201.

Flusser, Vilém, 2000, *Towards a Philosophy of Photography* (trans. Anthony Matthews). London: Reaktion Books.

Flusser, Vilém, 2013, *Post-History* (trans. Rodrigo Maltez-Novaes). Minneapolis: Univocal.

Farocki, Harun, 2004, 'Reality Would Have to Begin' in Elsaesser, Thomas (ed.), *Working on the Sightlines.* Amsterdam: Amsterdam University Press: 193–202.

Husserl, Edmund, 1983, *Ideas Pertaining to a Pure Phenomenology and to a Phenomenological Philosophy: First Book* (trans. F. Kersten). The Hague: Martinus Nijhoff.

Kelsey, Robin, 2011, 'Reverse Shot: Earthrise and Blue Marble in the American Imagination' in *New Geographies 4: Scales of the Earth.* Cambridge, MA: Harvard University Press: 10–16.

Kracauer, Siegfried, 1960, *Theory of Film: The Redemption of Physical Reality.* Oxford: Oxford University Press.

Maynard, Patrick, 2008, 'Scales of Space and Time in Photography: "Perception Points Two Ways"' in Walden, Scott (ed.), *Photography and Philosophy: Essays on the Pencil of Nature.* London: Blackwell: 187–209.

Merleau-Ponty, Maurice, 1968, 'Scale – Ontological significance of this notion' in *The Visible and the Invisible* (trans. Alphonso Lingis). Evanston, Ill.: Northwestern University Press: 226–227.

Nancy, Jean-Luc, 2005, *The Ground of the Image* (trans. Jeff Fort). Stanford, CA: Stanford University Press.

Osborne, Peter, 2011, 'Expecting the Unexpected: Beyond the "Horizon of Expectation"' in Hlavajova, Maria, Simon Sheikh and Jill Winder (eds.), *On Horizons: A Critical Reader in Contemporary Art.* Utrecht and Rotterdam: BAK & Post Editions: 113–128.

Osborne, Peter, 2014, *Anywhere or Not at All: Philosophy of Contemporary Art.* London: Verso.

Ricoeur, Paul, 2004, *Memory, History, Forgetting* (trans. Kathleen Blamey and David Pellaeur). Chicago and London: University of Chicago Press.

Sekula, Allan, 1986, 'The Body and the Archive' in *October* 39 (Winter): 3–64.

Sheikh, Simon, 2011, 'Vectors of the Possible: Art Between Spaces of Expectation and Horizons of Expectation' in Hlavajova, Maria, Simon Sheikh and Jill Winder (eds.), *On Horizons: A Critical Reader in Contemporary Art.* Utrecht and Rotterdam: BAK & Post Editions: 152–166.

Sontag, Susan, 1979, *On Photography.* London and New York: Penguin Books.

Steyerl, Hito, 2011, 'In Free Fall: A Thought Experiment' in Hlavajova, Maria, Simon Sheikh and Jill Winder (eds.) *On Horizons: A Critical Reader in Contemporary Art.* Utrecht and Rotterdam: BAK & Post Editions: 168–190.

Steyerl, Hito, 2012, *The Wretched of the Screen.* Berlin: Sternberg Press.

Stiegler, Bernard, 2009, *Technics and Time 2: Disorientation.* Stanford CA: Stanford University Press.

Virilio, Paul, 1994, *The Vision Machine* (trans. Julie Rose). Bloomington: Indiana University Press.

Weizman, Eyal, 2012, *The Least of All Possible Evils: Humanitarian Violence from Arendt to Gaza.* London and New York: Verso.

Wells, Rachel, 2013, 'Photography, Sculpture and Scale' in *Scale in Contemporary Sculpture: Enlargement, Miniaturization and the Life-Size.* Farnham: Ashgate: 119–160.

Andrew Fisher is a Lecturer in Visual Cultures at Goldsmiths, University of London and founding editor of the journal *Philosophy of Photography*. His recent publications include *On the Verge of Photography: Imaging Beyond Representation* (co-edited with Daniel Rubinstein & Johnny Golding, Article Press, Birmingham, 2013). He is currently working on two projects. The first is a book-length study of the interrelated technical, phenomenological, geographical and political senses of 'scale' in and for photography and the second is *Visual Cultures as Document* (a book co-authored with Nicole Wolf, Sternberg Press).

Sarine Waltenspül

The Camera as a Scaling Instrument: Focus on Cinematographic Modelling Techniques

Sarine Waltenspül

The Camera as a Scaling Instrument: Focus on Cinematographic Modelling Techniques

In filmic practice, different scaling techniques are used in different areas. Thus, for example, the production budget can be reduced, photographic and film material can be copied to a larger format with the help of the so-called blow-up method, whereby the material can show a close-up of a smiling face that is subsequently projected on to a cinema screen so that it appears larger than life size. These are all forms of scaling that this essay will *not* address. For alongside scaling techniques used in the shooting or the image composition (close-up[1]), when writing or editing the film material (blow-up[2]), or for the reproduction or playback (the size of the screen or the monitor, as well as the size of the projected image content)[3], I would like to suggest that scaling techniques exist that occupy an intermediate position between shooting, editing and playback. I include in these the modelling techniques that will now be the focus of this essay.

The main aim of this article is to clarify the role of the camera in work with cinematographic models and associated modelling techniques. My hypothesis is that this role consists of scaling processes in which the camera acts as a scaling instrument.[4] Before this hypothesis is pursued, some

1 Doane (2003) and Doane (2013). See also 'Visions of Scale: Magnification, Duration, Perspective, Projection', *Ninth Annual Graduate Student Conference*, Department of Cinema and Media Studies University of Chicago, 5–6 April 2013.

2 A prominent filmic negotiation of the technique is found in Michelangelo Antonioni's *Blow-Up* (UK/I 1966).

3 Cf. Souriau (1951). Souriau initially presented his idea in a course at the Institut de Filmologie during the 1950/51 semester. His speech was originally published as 'La structure de l'univers filmique et le vocabulaire de la filmologie' in Souriau (1951: 231–240).

4 It should be noted that the concept of the camera is used heuristically here. It stands for a complex apparatus whose parts and functions (lens, aperture, shutter, film material, etc.) are worth analysing individually in terms of their scaling qualities, but this cannot be done

conceptual and theoretical foundations need to be discussed that concern cinematographic models. In doing so, I would like to show in particular why cinematographic objects occupy an *intermediate position* between two 'modes of existence', as they are both actually existing material objects that are worked with during the production phase of a film, as well as medially conveyed objects that appear to the viewer projected on an arbitrary surface. Only after the cinematographic models are systematised can one answer the question of how the scaled models can become the illusions that appear on the cinema screen. Thus this article investigates illusionary-simulative models under the aspect of size scaling. Furthermore, owing to space constraints I will restrict myself to static models filmed from a fixed camera.[5]

Cinematographic modelling techniques as scaling techniques

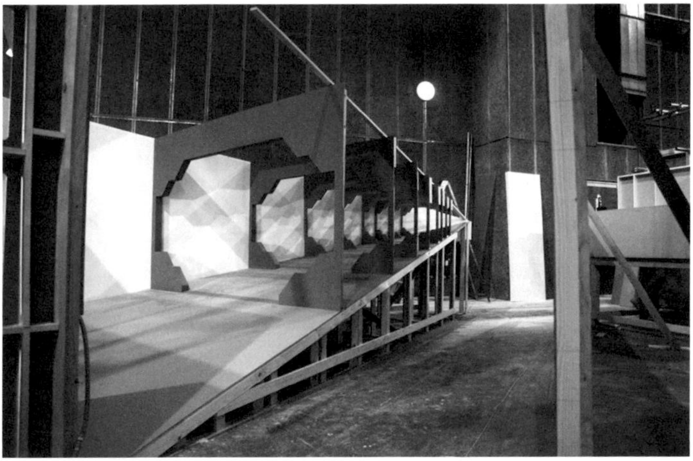

Fig. 1: Forced perspective set, Moon (UK 2009, director: Duncan Jones), (Copyright © Gavin J. Rothery, www.gavinrothery.com).

here due to spatial constraints. As opposed to the camera *in toto*, which I view as "technical medium" in Sybille Krämer's sense, given that I focus on size scaling [in this essay], I would like to define it 'merely' as a "technical instrument" here and explicitly not as a "technical medium" (cf. Krämer 1998: 73–94). This focus is also the reason why I will not go further here into the discourse on so-called apparatus theory (cf. e.g. Baudry 1974–75).

5 By contrast, models can be mobile (e.g. scaled bodies, cars or miniature explosions and the like) and the camera itself can be moving, as it is the case for example with the model shots for *2001: A Space Odyssey* (US/UK 1968, director: Stanley Kubrick), from which subsequently with *Star Wars Episode IV: A New Hope* (US 1977, director: George Lucas) the technique of motion control was developed enabling tracking shots to be repeated, whereby background and moving model could be combined.

The film examples I am working with stem from narrative cinema, which is viewed in contrast to documentary, nature, or art films. My point of departure is Duncan Jones' science-fiction film Moon (UK 2009), which is of particular interest owing to the modelling and scaling techniques used in it. The feature film debut of the British director was realised with a relatively small budget of 5 million USD (Shay 2009: 12) and shot at Shepperton Studios in southern England, where for example Ridley Scott's *Alien* (UK 1979) was also shot, in which models were used almost excessively (Arnold 2010: 35).[6] Thirty years later, Jones responded to an interviewer's question of whether this was by chance with "not completely" (Arnold 2010: 35). For in *Moon* models were used for the exterior shots that were made under the guidance of the model maker Bill Pearson and that were filmed under that of Cinesite's visual effects supervisor Simon Stanley-Clamp (Shay 2009: 12). Jones reports:

> Shooting this mixture of live-action and CG [computer-generated], meant that we could get the most bang for the buck and create something that had a lot of texture. We could give the film a real sense of epic scale, but at the same time be able to capture as much in-camera as possible. (Shay 2009: 12)

Hence at a time when production of computer-generated images (CGI) has become everyday filmic practice – and particularly for science-fiction films – Jones opted to mostly use techniques developed in the previous century. For the CGI effects are reduced to a minimum: thus, for example, the moon dust was generated afterwards (Shay 2009: 18), and Gerty, the nonhuman robot, was partially animated subsequently (Shay 2009: 14).

The in-camera effects mentioned by Jones are effects that arise *in* the camera instead of such effects that are achieved afterwards, when the film material is edited in post-production, which includes both analogue and digital editing. Among these in-camera effects are all those visual effects that arise *during* filming and *without* subsequent manipulation of the material (Rickitt 2007: 372), for example time-lapse and slow motion, change-over, (analogue) matte painting, rear projection and front projection, the slit-scan method, forced perspective and the Schüfftan method of

6 H.R. Giger, Carlo Rambaldi, Brian Johnson, Nick Adler und Denys Ayling received the Academy Award for Visual Effects in *Alien* in 1980. Online at: http://awardsdatabase.oscars.org/ampas_awards/DisplayMain.jsp?curTime=1439067388148 (accessed 30 January 2017). The effects in *Alien* were handled so convincingly that the special effects magazine *Cinefex* devoted a large part of the 1980 edition to the film – it was the very first edition of *Cinefex* (cf. *Cinefex*, No. 1, March 1980).

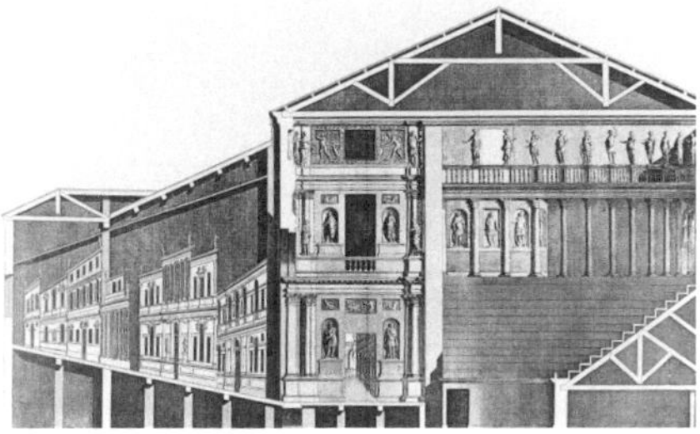

Fig. 2: Cutaway drawing of the Teatro Olimpico, woodcut by Ottavio Berotti Scamozzi, 1790 (Beyer 2009).

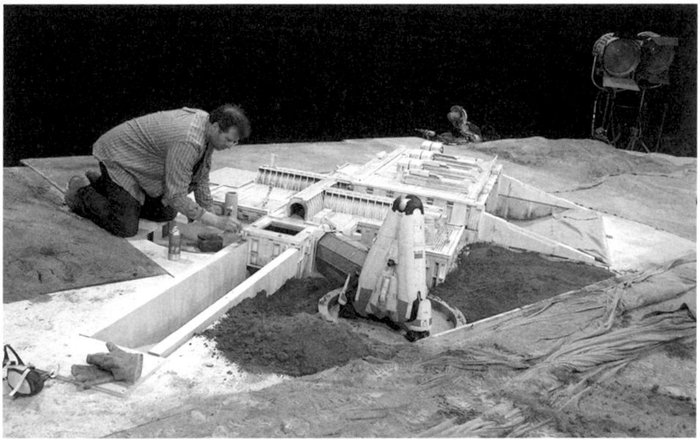

Fig. 3: Profilmic model, Moon (UK 2009, director: Duncan Jones) (Copyright © Steve Howarth, modelminiatures.co.uk).

combining models with live action shots.[7] The two latter methods are carried out with the help of modelling techniques and work with scaled cinematographic models.

In *Moon*, one scene was shot with the help of a forced perspective set (fig. 3). Gavin Rothery, visual effects supervisor of TinkTank Studios, said it was a challenge to create an "infinitely long corridor for as little money as possible in a small corner of the set" (Rothery 2011). His suggestion of solving the problem with two mirrors with whose help the endless corridor could be simulated could not be realized because such large mirrors would have been too expensive. They then resorted to a forced perspective set (Rothery 2011).

7 More on the Schüfftan method can be found in Vana (2001).

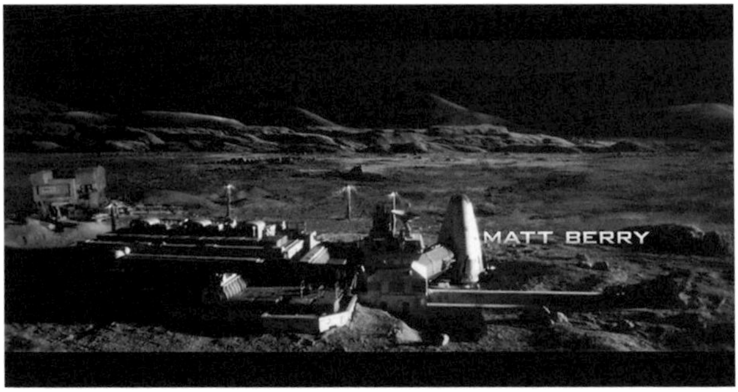

Fig. 4: Screenic model, Moon (UK 2009, director: Duncan Jones).

In the following I would like to show that the representation technique used to create a forced perspective was not initially developed for film. My hypothesis is that filmmakers make use of a stage-architectural representation technique that dates back to the Renaissance. A significant example is the Teatro Olimpico of Andrea Palladio in Vicenza, which opened in 1585. The stage architecture was designed by Vincenzo Scamozzi, who completed the construction of the theatre after Palladio's death (fig. 4). The aisles leading from the main stage area show rows of houses from ancient Thebes mixed with contemporary buildings (Beyer 2009: 58). These were erected on the rising stage floor and are foreshortened toward the vanishing point. This scaling, which increases progressively from the front to the rear area, creates a heightened impression of depth. As always with such trompe-l'œil representations that build on central projection, there is an ideal, monocular viewing perspective from which the illusion works most convincingly. If the viewer moves from this ideal eye point ('eye' in the singular!), the illusion fades.

These prerequisites are the ideal basis for a transfer of the technique to the filmic area. In a forced perspective, differently scaled elements are used, which is why such sets are also called mixed scale sets (Hutchison 1987: 20). The scaling of the parts, which can consist of models or of two-dimensional elements (e.g. painted scenery),[8] increases with growing distance to the camera.

Examples include *Moon* and *Metropolis* (Germany 1927, director: Fritz Lang), which I will return to later and the kitchen scene in Michel Gondry's *Eternal Sunshine of the Spotless Mind* (US 2004). In the latter, Joel, who has 'shrunk' to the size of a child, hides under a table, where Clementine looks

8 For details, see Vana (2001).

for him. The size difference between the two adult actors was realized based on a set whose elements – unlike in the case of *Moon* – do not get smaller as the distance from the camera increases, but larger. On account of this perspectival distortion, Clementine in the front (unscaled) picture area looks like an adult and Joel in the rear (scaled) area like a child.

Cinematographic model types

Before focusing in more detail on the relationship between camera and scaled film-set buildings, I would like to clarify a few conceptual and systematic foundations.

On the term scaling: Scaling comes from the Italian word *scala* which means 'step, stair, gradation' and is based on the Latin term *scandere* meaning 'to climb'. However, since around 1700 it has mainly been used in a figurative sense and particularly in technical fields denotes a 'graduated scale'.[9] *Scaling* is generally understood as meaning a change of size. Admittedly mass, time and temperature can also be scaled. In the context of this article, however, scaling means the change of size relations.

On the difference between 'model' and 'miniature': These two terms are closely related in the filmic context as well as in other contexts, there are often no fixed rules for differentiating the two. According to the author and model-maker Nicholas Seldon, the technical term in filmic practice is *model*. In his text with the somewhat misleading title *Gulliver in* Hollywood*: The World of Movie Miniatures* he stresses that "pros" call their objects "models", not "miniatures" (Seldon 1983: 88).[10]

On the systemisation of cinematographic models in two steps: In a *first step* I would like to differentiate models worked with in the production phase and that exist as scaled models from those that finally appear on the screen. In so doing, I would like to make use of Etienne Souriau's terminology[11] with which he divides up the "filmic universe" into "seven levels of existence" (Souriau 1951: 234), of which two are significant here: the "profilmic" and the "screenic." In Souriau's terminology, scaled models found in a set correspond to the "profilmic" objects, while those that are medially conveyed correspond to "screenic" ["écranique"] objects. Souriau describes the profilmic as "every objective reality that is to be filmed, especially everything that was created or arranged specifically for this purpose" (Souriau 1951: 240; original in French). The screenic denotes that which "can be observed on the screen during the projection of the film" (Souriau 1951: 240;

9 Entry "Skala" in *Etymologisches Wörterbuch des Deutschen* (2012: 1298).
10 In older film technique books, however, the term *miniature* is found.
11 On the history of the reception of Souriau's terminology cf. Kessler (1996).

original in French). This includes perception of the screen itself, which is illustrated by his example of the changing size with the increasing distance or closeness of the viewer to the screen. Transferred to the examples from *Moon*, the scaled moon basis which was used on the set corresponds to the profilmic model (fig. 1), whereas the model projected after the shooting was completed is the screenic one (fig. 2).

The *second step* for systemization can be found in my analysis of the heterogeneous cinematographic models, which I subdivide as follows:[12] (1) illusionary-simulative models, (2) stylistic or non-simulative models, (3) motivic-cinematographic models and (4) transfilmic models. *Illusionary-simulative models* (1) are used in film when their reference object is not available, does not exist, or when it cannot be dealt with as desired (when for example a building is to be blown up). They are inextricably entwined with the modelling techniques corresponding to them, which make them illusions to begin with. These include, for instance, perspectival distortions and the manipulation of the frame rate, to which I will return. Thus with the help of the techniques the models simulate reference objects and hence suggest the illusion of size and mass.[13] The illusionary-simulative models veil their existence as models in the projection; they are not recognizable as such. This group of models probably encompasses – alongside the motivic models – most of the models that occur in films in the one way or the other. Unlike the first, the *stylistic or non-simulative models* (2) do not veil their existence as models, but rather show this more or less explicitly and 'reveal' the conditions of the illusion. This 'failure' of the illusion cannot be attributed to faulty implementation, but is apparent, set up and recognizable as such. So the stylistic models are linked with the modelling techniques and can thus suggest size and mass, but do so *as models*, which undermines the perfect illusion. The *motivic models* (3) do not claim to be illusory and, unlike the first two groups, exist irrespective of the cinematographic modelling techniques. Cinematographic models can be viewed as motifs when they appear as objects which in their specific scaling and their materiality are integrated in the filmic-diegetic activity. They appear *as models* in the film.[14] The group of *transfilmic models* (4) encompasses cinematographic models and modelling techniques that transcend their original context –

12 This stems from my engagement with cinematographic models within the framework of my dissertation.

13 So when judging the persuasiveness of these models it is necessary to check whether the illusion functions or not, taking into account that viewing habits may have been historically conditioned.

14 This kind of model is discussed for example in *Mock-ups in Close-up* by Gabu Heindl and Drehli Robnik. More on Heindl and Robnik's project on mock-ups in close-up in Heindl and Robnik (2008), Heindl and Robnik (2012) and Heindl and Robnik (2014).

the specific film or the medium of film – and develop a kind of life of their own. This is the case, for example, when models are transferred to the exhibition context or become the basis of a computer game, as in the case of *Lumino City,* which was filmed completely in a handmade model and into which the figures were rendered afterwards. In this case, stylistic elements of the cinematographic models were transferred to the game.

In this essay, I will restrict myself to the illusionary-simulative models, among which those in *Moon* can be counted.[15] My suggestion as to what they have to do with scaling is as follows: they are objects that undergo a *shift of scale* twice, namely (a) when they are made and (b) when they are filmed. In the first case (a) I see the material, actual, profilmic models in a scaling relationship to their real or fictive reference object, in other words to a full-scale object.[16] In terms of their planning and creation, these models are scaled in relation to this full-scale object. However, profilmic models not only stand in a scaling relationship to their real or fictive full-scale reference object, but also to the film frame (b), insofar as the second scale shift occurs in the course of the media translation process, by which both the film and the playback of what is filmed are meant. With the help of the appropriate camera and set techniques, the scaled model is filmed such that it appears as a full-scale object on the screen/monitor. Thus with the illusionary-simulative models at issue are objects whose original size is veiled by the way in which they are projected. Rolf Brenzen refers to the models Leon Battista Alberti uses to plan his buildings as "three-dimensional representatives of the intended original" (Brenzen 1986: 165, cf. also Wendler 2013: 80). I would also like to view the cinematographic models as such 'three-dimensional representatives of an intended original'.

Cinematographic models as double objects

At this point I would like to put forward the hypothesis that cinematographic models constitute contradictory objects in the terminology of a binary logical system. For they are actually not one, but *two* objects that are also *the same* object. A fruitful approach for supporting my hypothesis can be found in Lorenz Engell's and André Wendler's conception of the "double object" (Engell and Wendler 2009 and 2011: 29). In their research on motifs, Engell and Wendler call film motifs "double objects" and go on to write that these always appear "in a double temporality", namely, in the

15 It should be noted that a motivic model was also used in *Moon*, namely in the form of a carved model of the city of Fairfield. Based on the model, the two Sams notice that not only their outer appearance is identical, but that they also share the same memories (of Fairfield).

16 They are mostly models *of* something, and were thus created retrospectively. However, in science fiction films in particular there are often models of objects that do not exist or do not exist *yet*.

"perfect [of their] production *and* in the present [of their] projection" (Engell and Wendler 2011: 29. Emphasis in original). Transferred to the (model) basis from *Moon* this means that as a profilmic model it is in the mode of the perfect of its production (fig. 1) and as a screenic model in the mode of the present of its projection (fig. 2). Hence Wendler and Engell's approach can also be made fruitful for cinematographic models that do *not* necessarily occur as motifs in films, as for example the illusionary-simulative and the stylistic models. In this context, I would like to extrapolate on the concept of the double object. Profilmic illusionary-simulative and stylistic models are always also conceived and built as screenic objects from the outset. In the screenic stylistic models, the associated profilmic model even continues to be recognizable. In both cases the modelling techniques are taken into consideration. Thus the models exist not only in a material (profilmic) and in a media (filmic) state, but in their respective state also refer to the respective other: in the profilmic-simulative model the screenic illusion is always considered, and a filmic-stylistic model reveals that it exists as a (material, profilmic) model. The cinematographic models are therefore not simply double objects that exist in the perfect of their production and in the present of their projection. Rather, insofar as through their state they refer to the other state, they 'contain' both, as it were. From this I would like to draw the conclusion that they are both one object and two. The statement that a cinematographic model is both one object and two must be viewed as being invalid in a binary operating system, like the ones that prevail in most logics and in language, and thus in thought. Therefore here I would like to argue for a truth system of multi-valued logic,[17] enabling the possibilities of understanding to be extended. An example of such a multi-valued logical system is Nuel Belnap's four-valued logic (1977). This logic does not merely operate with the binary truth values 't' for true and 'f' for false, but also with the values 'n' for none and 'b' for both. This has the advantage that it "knows how to deal with both contradictory and missing information" (Weber 1998: i).[18] Based on Belnap's fourvalued logic, I would

17 More on multi-valued logic systems in Kreiser, Gottwald and Stelzner (1987) and Günter (1971).

18 Comparable approaches can of course be found not only in logic but also in various other areas. Here I would like to refer to two relatively contemporary examples: John Law's concept of "fractional coherence" in STS (*science and technology studies*) and Jean-Luc Nancy's "being singularly plural" in philosophy. In his *Aircraft Stories*, Law counters the dualisms of binary operating systems with the metaphor of fractionality: "Fractionality, then, is one of the possible metaphors for trying to avoid such dualisms. For trying to wrestle with the idea that objects, subjects and societies are both singular and multiple, both one and many. Both/and" (2002: 4). He continues: "Objects in the world [...] are more than one and less than many" (2002:194). By contrast, Nancy dispenses with the binary oppositional terms "singular" and "plural" and defines being as "singular and plural at once, indistinctly *and* distinctly." (Nancy 1996: 48, original in French, emphasis in the original).

like to suggest that the cinematographic objects/models are 'b', or 'both'. For they are both profilmic *and* screenic models, *and* also *both* at the same time. With this, I would like to return to the hypothesis expressed at the beginning of this essay, namely, that the camera plays a key role in filmic scaling processes and in them acts as a scaling instrument.

The camera as scaling instrument

According to Souriau, the camera is linked with its objects *per se*. He writes that "a peculiar part of this real or afilmic world is already geared strongly towards the filmological", referring particularly to things that are "put in front of the camera in a purposeful way" (Souriau 1951: 235, original in French). Furthermore, he says that the profilmic, or the profilmic object, is often "created only with respect to its functional role" (Souriau 1951: 235, original in French), and that "the totality of operations in the shooting (which are profilmic: above all the camera, and this is particularly important, belongs to the profilmic) lead up to the image on the film strip" (Souriau 1951: 236, original in French). Thus according to Souriau not only are many profilmic objects created functionally, but their function consists precisely in being captured by the camera, which belongs to the same "level of existence" as the objects themselves: namely the profilmic. The camera has to be viewed as being constitutive for the functioning of the illusion; it and the scaled cinematographic models belong together. But how are the scaling qualities of the camera manifested?

In the transition from profilmic to filmic models, leaps take place regarding various modes: on the level of materiality, mediality, dimensionality and size. My hypothesis is that the conditions for the possibilities of size scaling lie in the nexus between camera and model. In turn, this nexus can be subdivided, for shifts in scale and can be produced both with the help of spatial (as for example in the case of forced perspective sets) and with the help of temporal arrangements or rearrangements. In a temporal respect, the camera acts as a scaling instrument for mobile models because it scales the size via the detour of time. For moving cinematographic models are filmed and played back with a manipulated frame rate.[19]

19 Nigel Stone, *director of photography* (DOP) of *model unit* for various films, illustrates this problem based on a simple example: "If you film a moving full-sized car at 24 frames it will look normal, but if you film a model car at 24 frames it will look like a toy car. That's because of the difference between the scale of its size and the scale of its weight." (Nigel Stone quoted in Rickitt 2007: 116.) The difference between the ratio of the mass and size of the model, and of the mass and size of the intended object on the screen, should be eliminated with the help of mathematical formulas for calculating the frame rate. The formulas stem from a discussion carried out in the 1920s and early 1930s within the framework of the *Society of Motion Picture Engineers* (cf. Ball 1924, Hutchins 1930) and subsequently included in relevant cinematic technique reading (e.g. Fielding 1985, Hutchison 1987, Rickitt 2007). They suggest precision

But now I would like to return to size scaling, where the following questions arise: What happens during the transition from physical models to medially conveyed models? What are the decisive factors in this second shift of the scale of the cinematographic models? And how do the scaled, profilmic models become the illusions on the cinema screen?

The *Moon* model maker Pearson reports that he was shocked when he learned that the stage on which the models were to be filmed was much smaller than expected.[20] In film history, there are countless such anecdotes about how the expected set constellations were smaller than had been anticipated, which often also had consequences for the models. Another striking example is *Metropolis*. Contrary to expectations, the "big shopping street", one the most prominent scenes in the film, had to be filmed in the small glass house in Babelsberg (Vana 2001: 169). This necessitated that the already produced (hand-drawn) designs had to be adapted, as is shown by the quote from Erich Kettelhut, who created the stage set:

> The only way to achieve the effects of size and depth shown in the design was to build the model, like the one for the Rhine Valley of the Nibelungen earlier on, with a marked perspectival foreshortening. Thus the stage set design drawings I had already finished were obsolete. (Vana 2001: 169–170)

Hence in the case of *Metropolis*, too, a forced perspective set was used as a solution for the spatial problem.[21] Gerhard Vana describes the role the camera plays here as follows:

> With a suitable camera location such a spatial reproduction can be implemented to create an illusion, because as opposed to immediate observation there is no contradiction between eye point and two-eyed viewing. (Vana 2001: 170)

While this representation technique was not developed genuinely for film, the imperfection that occurs in "immediate observation", as Vana

and security in the undertaking of translating scaled models 'correctly' into the intended illusions. Cf. Waltenspül (2015).

20 The new stage measured approximately 12 by 8 metres, and as a result the moon basis and some of the vehicles had to be created at a scale of 1:12. The close-ups of the vehicles were taken using models at a scale of 1:6. (Shay 2009: 17) Pearson goes on to say that they are "really tiny" (Pearson quoted in Shay 2009: 17). The scale of 1:12 corresponds to one inch to the foot in the Anglo-American measuring system.

21 More on the foreshortened stage-set buildings in *Metropolis* can be found in the excellent analysis by Gerhard Vana (2001).

argues, does not occur in the interplay with the (film) camera. For the camera can be the exact eye point, which does not deviate from the ideal location and which as opposed to a physically present viewer does not expose the illusion on account of two-eyed viewing. David Hutchison, the author of various texts and books on special effects, formulates the advantage of the monocular camera vis-à-vis binocular viewing somewhat less euphemistically than Vana: "In fact, the greater the mixture of scales used to force the perspective, the closer we get to having only one usable camera position" (Hutchison 1987: 20). So while the camera on the one hand is the suitable mediating authority as it does not work in a binocular way and thus represents the ideal eye point, on the other hand, this condition limits the choice in camera positioning to just one possible position. If this ideal constellation is achieved, neither the camera nor what it films can be moved. For in a perspectively oriented forced perspective set, no "adumbrations"[22] are possible, in Edmund Husserl's words. There is only *one* view, *one* "partial intention".[23] Hence forced perspective sets are themselves partial intentions, in a sense, with which, however – if central perspective laws are adhered to – a "total intention" (Husserl 1901: 513) can be suggested.

So Husserl's description of the genesis of an everyday perception also applies perfectly to a forced perspective set: what "viewed from the one side was only a visual intimation, from the other bwecomes a confirming and fully sufficient perception", or what "was only slightly hinted at, on this [side] comes at least to a pictorial intimation, it appears perspectively foreshortened and adumbrated, and will appear 'exactly the way it is' only from a new side" (Husserl 1901: 513). For the viewer, the endless corridor in *Moon* (fig. 3) is not a "thing" but merely "part of a thing" or a "moment" (Husserl 1901: 513) which as such can only be convincing from the one single camera perspective. In this context, these parts of things or moments lack what is proper to the perception of other, more everyday objects: the "possibility of an unlimited number of perceptions, differing in content, of a single object" (Husserl 1901: 528), which can only take form in the mind via the temporal succession of such 'moments'.

This 'imperfection' arising from the fact that the camera is limited to one perspective can be exploited more productively in film productions,

22 According to Husserl, the total perception of an object consists of the partial perception of it, which Husserl calls "Abschattung" (adumbration), arguing that any view at the same time excludes other views, i.e. 'eclipses' them.

23 "Nach unserer Auffassung ist jede Wahrnehmung und Imagination ein Gewebe von Partialintentionen, verschmolzen zur Einheit einer Gesammtintention [sic]. Das Correlat dieser Letzteren ist das Ding, während die Correlate jener Partialintentionen dingliche Theile und Momente sind." (Husserl 1901: 513).

because the exclusion of other possible views of the sets is also the condition for the possibility of representing the forced perspective set and scaling the elements to begin with. For only under this prerequisite is it possible to change the scale of the objects and to reduce their dimensions. With model ensembles as in the case of mixed scale sets, the different scales thus become stabilized in reference to the camera or the eye point.

In this essay I have worked out the extent to which the camera is linked with its objects and the extent to which this link, as soon as it concerns scaled objects, has to be seen as being constitutive for the functioning of filmic illusions. Thus the camera model nexus comprises the very conditions for size scaling, which would have to be differentiated in a further step. For the spatial arrangement alone – as in the case of the perspectively organised forced perspective sets – merely enables static arrangements (models and camera) to be scaled. As soon as movement comes into play, the requirements placed on the camera become more complex. Furthermore, my description of the camera as scaling instrument has consequences that touch on non-cinematic areas. For example, the question arises as to the role of the camera in scientific-experimental settings that use its effect on scale. Hence not only filmic fictions result from the camera model nexus, but also outcomes which, noticed or unnoticed, literally have a larger-*scale* effect on our everyday world.

English translation by Burke Barrett

References

Arnold, Frank, 2010, 'Klassisch verhaltenes Kammerspiel' in *Filmbulletin* 5(10): 34–36.

Ball, Joseph A., 1924, 'Theory of Mechanical Miniatures in Cinematography' in *Transactions of SMPE* 18 (May): 119–126.

Baudry, Jean-Louis, 1974–75, 'Ideological Effects of the Basic Cinematographic Apparatus' (trans. A. Williams) in *Film Quarterly* 28(2): 39–47.

Belnap, Nuel D., 1977, 'A Useful Four-Valued Logic' in Dunn, J. Michael, and George Epstein (eds.), *Modern Uses of Multiple-Valued Logic*. Dordrecht and Boston: Reidel: 5–37.

Beyer, Andreas, 2009, *Andrea Palladio: Teatro Olimpico*. Berlin: Verlag Klaus Wagenbach (1987).

Brenzen, Rolf, 1986, *Die praktische und theoretische Konstitution des Modellverfahrens: Ein Beitrag zur Frühgeschichte der neuzeitlichen Wissenschaft*. Frankfurt a. M., Bern and New York: Peter Lang.

Doane, Mary Ann, 2003, 'The Close-Up: Scale and Detail in the Cinema' in *Differences* 14(3): 89–111.

Doane, Mary Ann, 2013, 'Scale and the Negotiation of 'Real' and 'Unreal' Space in the Cinema' in Nagib, Lúcia, and Cecília Mello (eds.), *Realism and the Audiovisual Media*. London: Palgrave Macmillan: 63–81 (2009).

Engell, Lorenz, and André Wendler, 2009, 'Medienwissenschaft der Motive' in *Zeitschrift für Medienwissenschaft* 1: 38–49.

Engell, Lorenz, and André Wendler, 2011, 'Motiv und Geschichte' in *Rabbit Eye – Zeitschrift für Filmforschung* 3: 24–40.

Etymologisches Wörterbuch des Deutschen, 2012, Koblenz: Edition Kramer (2010).

Fielding, Raymond, 1985, *The Technique of Special Effects Cinematography*. London and New York: Focal Press (1965).

Günter, Gotthard, 1971, 'Die Theorien der 'mehrwertigen' Logik' in *Philosophische Perspektiven* 3: 110–131.

Heindl, Gabu, and Drehli Robnik, 2008, 'The Mighty Model: Mock-Ups in Close-Up' in *Archis* 16: 38–42.

Heindl, Gabu, and Drehli Robnik, 2012, 'Maßstab und Macht' in Elser, Oliver, and Peter Cachola Schmal (eds.), *Das Architekturmodell: Werkzeug, Fetisch, Kleine Utopie* (exh. cat. Deutsches Architekturmuseum Frankfurt a. M.). Zurich: Scheidegger & Spiess: 57–59.

Heindl, Gabu, and Drehli Robnik, 2014, 'Mock-Ups in Close-Up: Architectural Models in Film 1919–2013' in Museum für Gegenwartskunst Siegen (ed.), *Was Modelle können: Eine kleine Geschichte des Architekturmodells in der zeitgenössischen Kunst* (exh. cat.). Cologne: Snoeck: 112–115.

Husserl, Edmund, 1901, *Logische Untersuchungen. Zweiter Teil: Untersuchungen zur Phänomenologie und Theorie der Erkenntnis*. Halle: Max Niemeyer.

Hutchins, G. F., 1930, 'Dimensional Analysis as an Aid to Miniature Cinematography' in *Journal of the Society of Motion Picture Engineers* 14(4): 377–383.

Hutchison, David, 1987, *Film Magic: The Art and Science of Special Effects*. London: Simon & Schuster.

Kessler, Frank, 1996, 'Etienne Souriau und das Vokabular der filmologischen Schule' in *montage AV* 6/2/1996: 132–139.

Krämer, Sybille, 1998, *Das Medium als Spur und als Apparat*. Frankfurt a. M.: Suhrkamp.

Kreiser, Lothar, Siegfried Gottwald and Werner Stelzner (eds.), 1987, *Nichtklassische Logik: Eine Einführung*. Berlin: Akademie-Verlag.

Law, John, 2002, *Aircraft Stories: Decentering the Object in Technoscience*. Durham and London: Duke University Press.

Nancy, Jean-Luc, 1996, *Être singulier pluriel*. Paris: Galilée.

Rickitt, Richard, 2007, *Special Effects: The History and Technique*. New York: Billboard Books.

Rothery, Gavin, 2011, 'I am a space clone and I sleep in a drawer…'.
Online at http://www.gavin-rothery.com/they-never-went-to-the-moon/2011/8/20/i-am-a-space-clone-and-i-sleep-in- a-drawer.html (accessed 30 January 2017).

Seldon, Nicholas, 1983, 'Gulliver in Hollywood: The World of Movie Miniatures' in *American Cinematographer* Nov: 87–92.

Shay, Estelle, 2009, 'Moon Madness' in *Cinefex* 118 (July): 10–20.

Souriau, Etienne, 1951, 'La structure de l'univers filmique et le vocabulaire de la filmologie' in *Revue internationale de Filmologie* 2(7–8): 231–240.

Vana, Gerhard, 2001, *Metropolis: Modell und Mimesis*. Berlin: Gebr. Mann Verlag.

Waltenspül, Sarine, 2015, 'Der Kosmos aus der Petrischale. Oder: Wie lässt das Ähnlichkeitsprinzip Universen entstehen?' in Jürgens, Anna-Sophie, and Tassilo Tesche (eds.), *LaborARTorium: Forschung im Denkraum zwischen Wissenschaft und Kunst. Eine Methodenreflexion*. Bielefeld: Transcript Verlag: 109–121.

Weber, Stefan, 1998, *Investigations in Belnap's Logic of Inconsistent and Unknown Information*. PhD Thesis. Leipzig: Universität Leipzig.

Wendler, Reinhard, 2013, *Das Modell zwischen Kunst und Wissenschaft*. Munich: Wilhelm Fink Verlag.

Sarine Waltenspül (*1986) works as a research assistant at the Research Focus in Transdisciplinarity of the Zurich University of the Arts. She is currently doing her doctorate in media studies at the University of Basel. She studied philosophy, art history and cultural analysis at the University of Basel, the University of Zurich and Humboldt University of Berlin.

Helmut Völter

Masanao Abe: The Movement of the Clouds at Fuji

Helmut Völter
Masanao Abe: The Movement of the Clouds at Fuji

In 1927, the Japanese physicist Masanao Abe set up a self-financed observatory with a view of Fuji. From the observatory, he directed his cameras at the mountain to record and analyse the shapes and movements of the clouds. In this contribution, I would like to introduce his work based on 20 pictures.

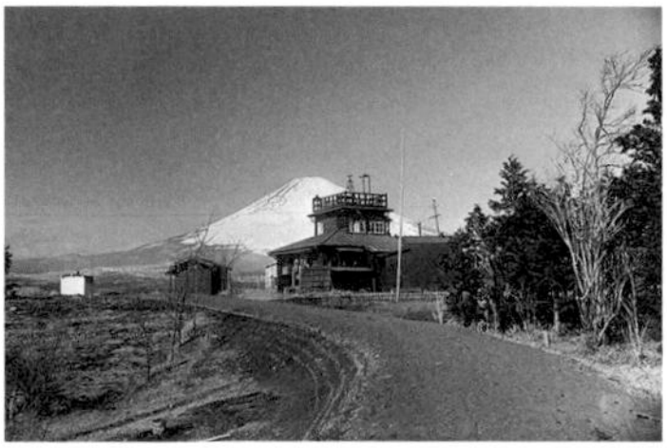

Abe's scientific project was to research the air currents at the mountain indirectly, based on the clouds. Film and photographic cameras were his most important tools. Abe was convinced that visual data sufficed to understand cloud movements. In parallel, he recorded meteorological standard values such as temperature and air pressure, but they hardly played a role in his scientific work. Nor was the weather or the season relevant for him. A model for Abe's studies was the French physiologist Étienne-Jules Marey, who like Abe was fascinated by movement and used photography as a central instrument for observation and analysis.

Scaling was a fundamental working method in the project. The photographic and filmic scaling of the mountain and the clouds on glass negatives and filmstrips was part of his analytical work: landscape and clouds could now be archived, measured and compared thanks to the radical simplification of a complex meteorological situation on a rectangular, black-and-white image section. Parallel to his observations at Fuji, Abe experimented in his Tokyo laboratory with a 1:10,000 model of Fuji in a wind tunnel: another scaling of the mountain to a practical room size.

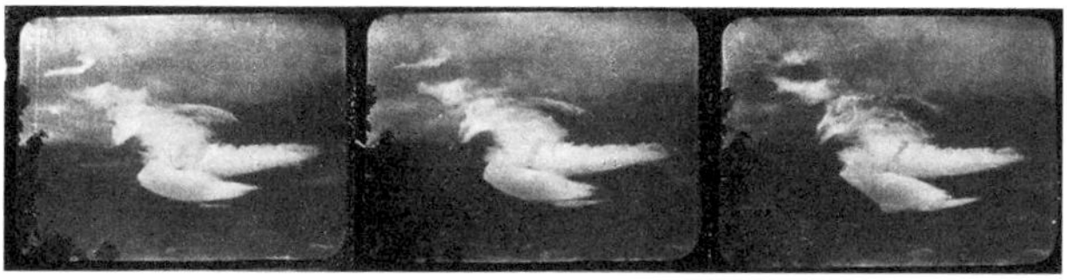

Abe's observatory was situated approximately 20 km southeast of Fuji. He had found the location a year previously. On 4 August 1926, he used a small handheld camera at the site to film a bizarre-shaped cloud that rotated around a vertical axis and simultaneously changed its shape. Its movements were too slow to be recognized with the naked eye – Abe only took a picture approximately every 10 seconds and used the images to create a time-lapse film. In his first scientific article, published in 1927 in Japanese and English, he analysed the cloud movements. He assumed that the surrounding mountains – including Fuji – were the reason that a wind current formed a vortex and thus twisted and deformed the cloud so impressively. He hypothesized that if one could interpret the shapes and movements of clouds correctly, one could understand the behaviour of the air currents that form them.

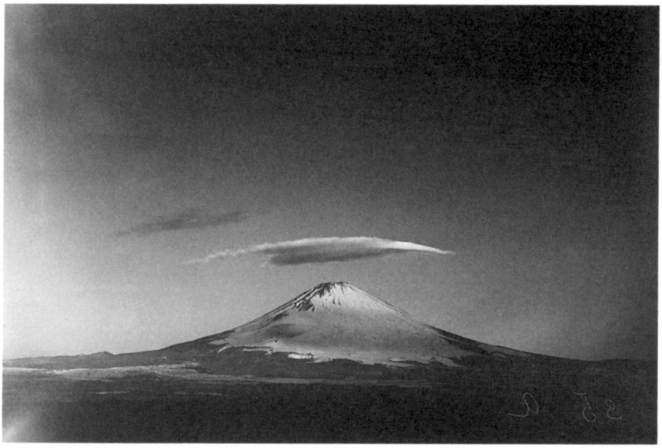

In this picture, photographed by Abe on 14 February 1933, 7:07 a.m., you see a special cloud shape, a kind of arc suspended above the peak of the mountain. It seems to leap across the summit. And this cloud is indeed formed by an air current flowing over the mountain. When the current is forced to rise and cools down, part of the water it contains condenses and the cloud forms.

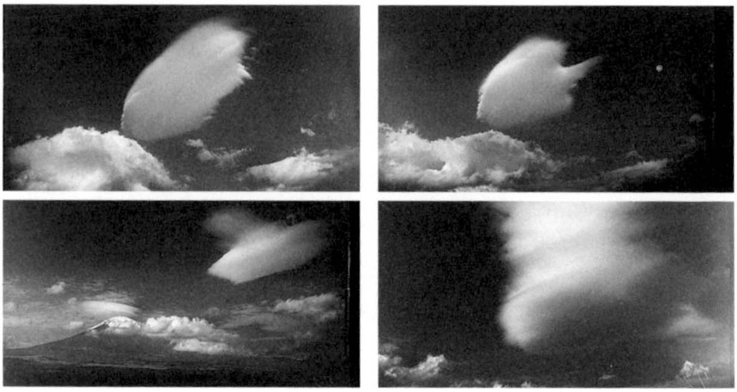

Abe photographed this four-part picture series on 13 November 1934 between 7:55 and 10:35 a.m. He published the very special cloud shape under the title "Tsurushi", a traditional Japanese name for these special clouds that only exist in the mountains.

Abe frequently used picture series to document developments in the sky. This was part of his sophisticated observation technique in which photography and film intertwine: Abe documented static situations that do not change over a longer period with individual pictures. He captured movements and changes of shape with the film camera, and he always used the pictures to create time-lapse movies. In most cases, he used film and photography in parallel: the plate camera had a much more detailed, sharply focused image, which supplemented the grainy and coarse 35-mm film shots.

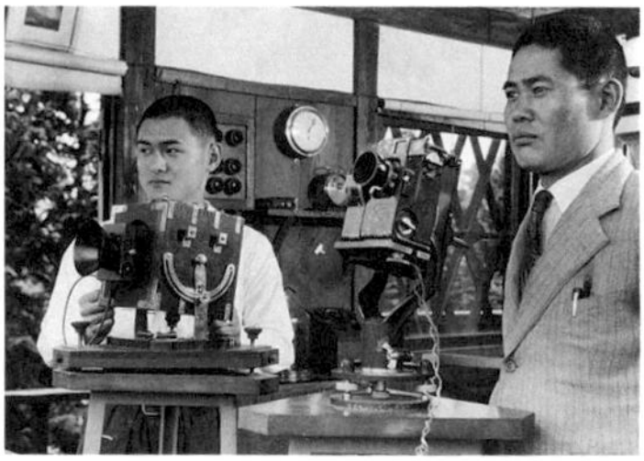

Two of Abe's assistants at work in the observatory. The large camera on the left is a plate camera, the smaller camera on the right is a film camera (a French Débrie Sept). As a member of the high nobility, Abe had the financial means not only to buy a large number of meteorological measuring instruments for his observatory, but also to employ his own assistants for the tedious observation work.

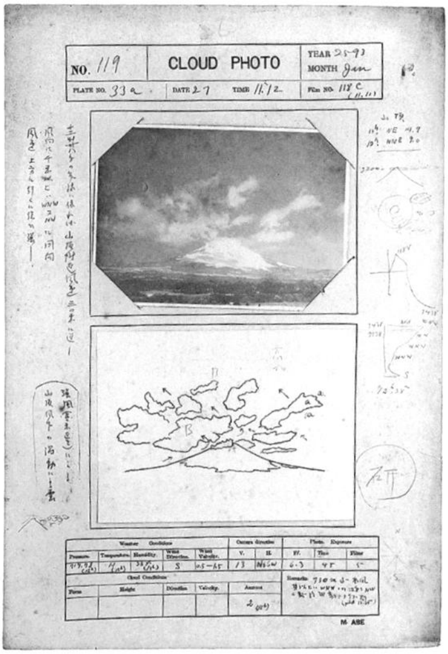

For his research, Abe used these self-developed large-scale forms to record his observations. Under the contact print of a photograph is a drawing, constituting the first step of his analysis. In it, he further reduced the photograph to the essential outlines of mountain and clouds and added the movement directions with arrows. This, too, is a kind of scaling.

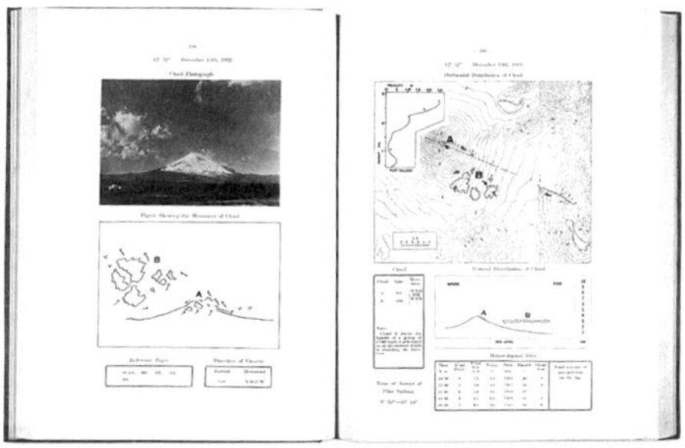

In 1937, Abe published the over 400-page book *Distribution and Movement of Cloud around Mt. Fuji Studied through Photographs*. Unlike in his scientific articles, in which he reported on the progress of his work and analysed air currents at the mountain, this book is purely a collection of data in which he revealed the results of his observations to enable other scientists to use them.

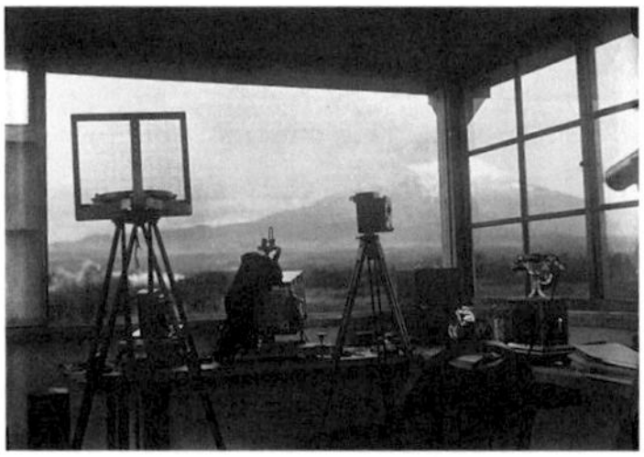

A picture of Abe's workplace: Two tripods stand behind a table like two people looking out of the window at the distant Fuji. The window frame on the right divides up the view of the landscape geometrically, as though to make it measurable.

One of Abe's first decisions was to always carry out his observations at the same point 20 kilometres away from the mountain. Only twice, in the summers of 1932 and 1937, did he ascend the mountain with cameras to film from there. His decision reflects a traditional aesthetic maxim according to which it is more valuable to view Fuji from a distance than to physically climb up to the peak. For the scientific evaluation of his data, it was essential that his pictures and films were taken from the same standpoint in identical conditions. Only then could they be compared. And there was another reason why Abe researched Fuji only from a distance: a view from afar permitted an overview, reducing the overabundance of details that would have overwhelmed researchers at the location.

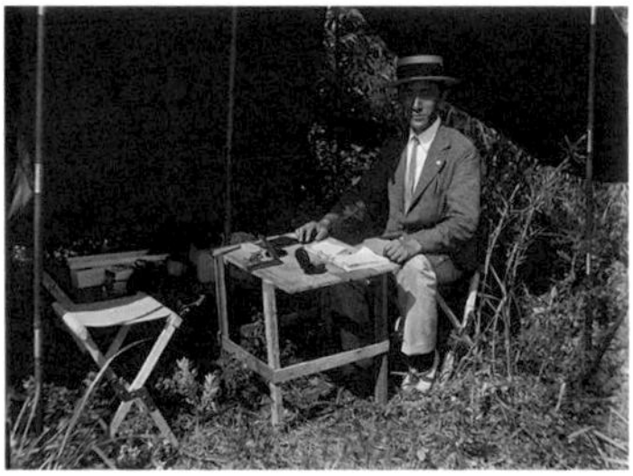

In this picture Abe is wearing elegant English clothing contrasting with the improvised wooden table in front of him. He is sitting in a tent that he and his assistants used for the observation work before the observatory was built. Abe's penchant for Western clothing and his good knowledge of English were the result of a one-year stay in London where he had gone with his wife after he had finished his studies in physics.

1933

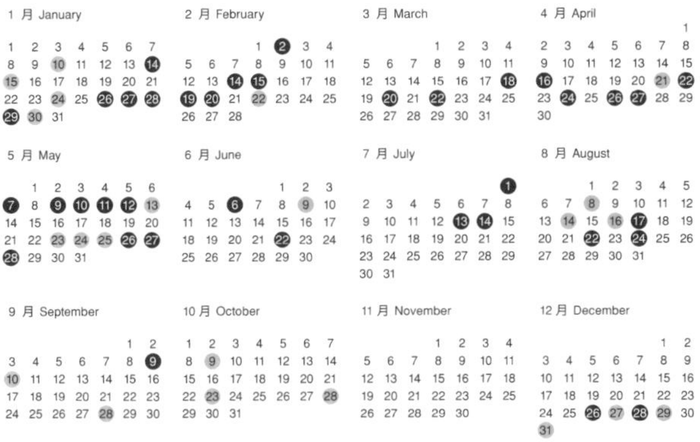

On this calendar page Abe's cloud work in 1933 is noted. A light gray dot stands for only one cloud photograph, a dark gray dot for more than one cloud photograph. We can see the extent to which the scientists' activity consisted above all of patient waiting! All too often, the sky was either cloud-free or too many clouds between the mountain and the observatory obstructed the view. Often, several days elapsed without a picture being taken.

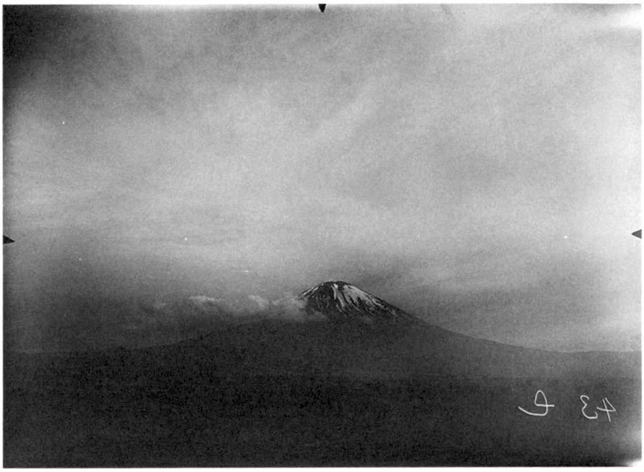

On 25 May 1933, amid a series of consecutive foggy days, Abe and his assistants only took one photograph at 8:56 a.m.

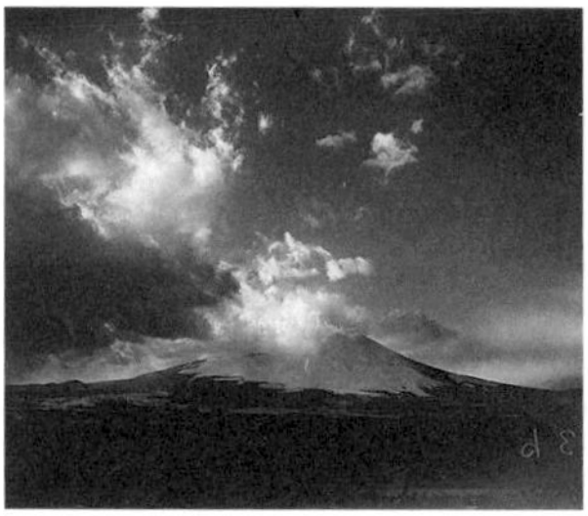
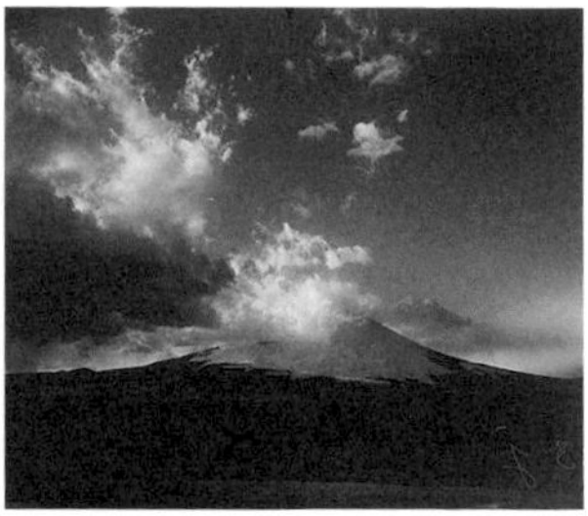

Masanao Abe did not photograph with one camera but with two, in order to obtain stereo image pairs (those shown here are photographed 13 December 1932, 12:52 p.m.). With a stereo view he could comprehend how the clouds stood in relation to the mountain. In the process, he used a method from surveying technology: the second camera did not stand right next to the first, but 500 metres away at a second station. This large distance enhanced the stereo effect making the spatial effect much stronger than a simple view of the sky could have done.

Once again, it becomes apparent how Abe's observation methods did not rely on an overly detailed recording of visible reality, but how a scaling and reduction were already established in the media arrangement. By means of stereo amplification and time lapse, Abe made the phenomena he studied visible to begin with in many cases.

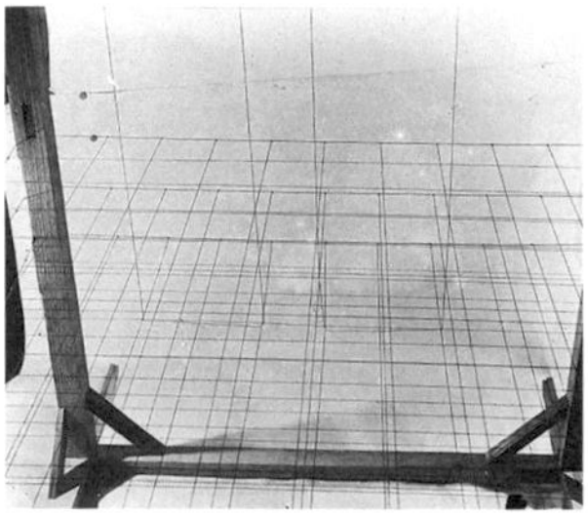
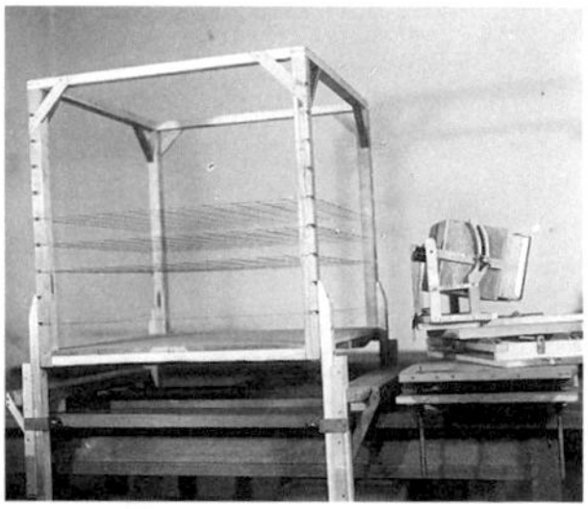

With the stereo pairs, Abe could not only look at the spatial conditions, but also calculate them. To this end, he constructed this three-dimensional grid of which he took a stereoscopic picture. He laid the image pair over a stereoscopic picture of clouds, creating the impression of a grid suspended in the landscape. With a little practice, it was possible to determine the height and geographical position of the clouds.

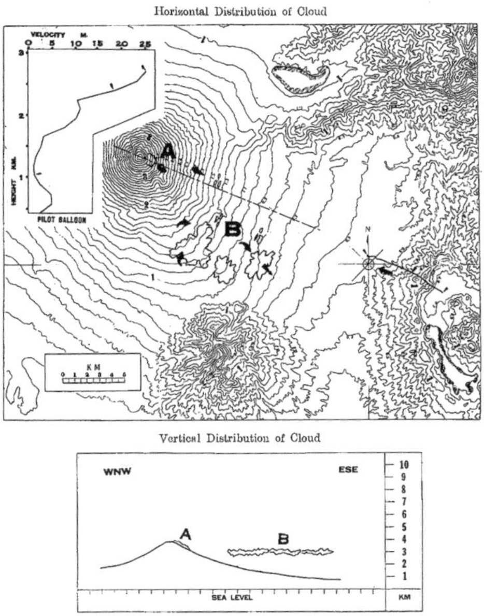

These maps, published in Abe's 1937 book, show the precision and detail of Abe's calculations. The upper map shows a bird's-eye view of the landscape and the clouds; the lower maps shows a cross-sectional view. They are based on the photographs taken on 13 December 1932.

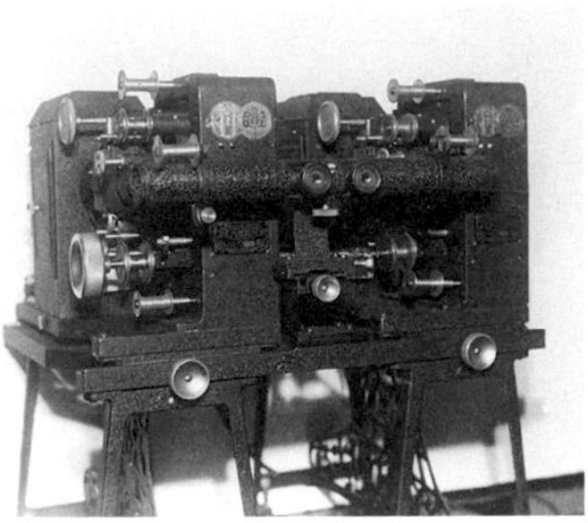

After a few attempts, in 1934 Abe was ready to use not only stereoscopic photographs, but also stereo films for his work. For this purpose, he constructed this viewer for stereo films that consisted of two synchronised projectors connected via mirrors.

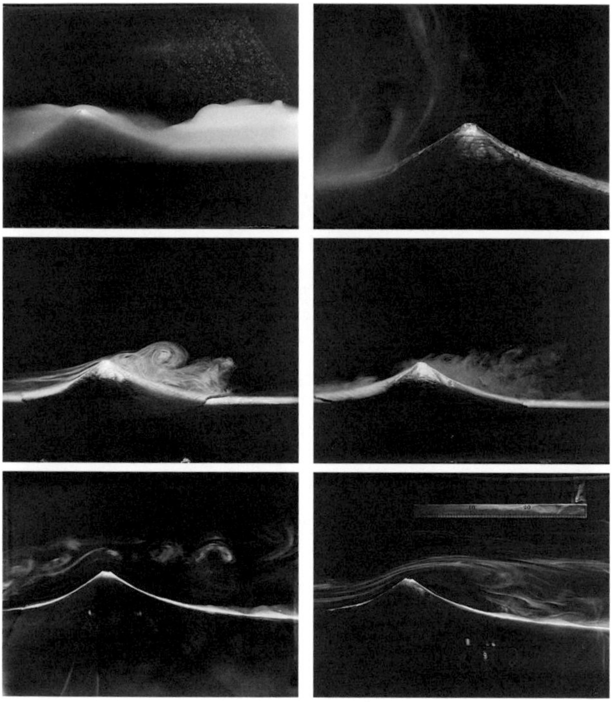

In addition to his research at Fuji, Abe supplemented his work with wind tunnel experiments in his house in Tokyo. A special interest of his was to study the behaviour of the wind also in a place where he could not observe any clouds. And just as his photographs and films previously had reduced Fuji to a manageable size, with his mountain model Abe created a further possibility of studying, within the dimensions of his lab, a landscape stretching out several kilometres.

At the end of the 1920s, when Abe undertook his first wind tunnel experiments, wind tunnels had long been a proven tool for constructing aircraft. However, no one had successfully tested an entire landscape in a wind tunnel, for the wind tunnel would have to be structurally adapted: while for an aircraft only a uniform current has to be simulated, in a landscape winds, temperature, air pressure, etc. can differ substantially at different heights. Abe assumed that the collision of winds from different directions and with different intensities is decisive for the behaviour of air currents at Fuji and tried to reproduce this experimentally.

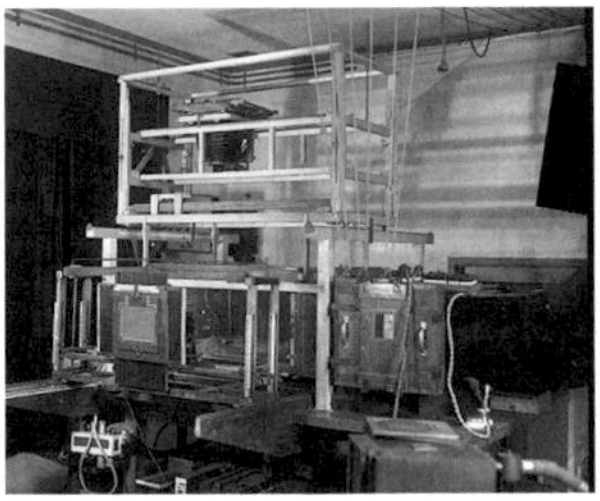

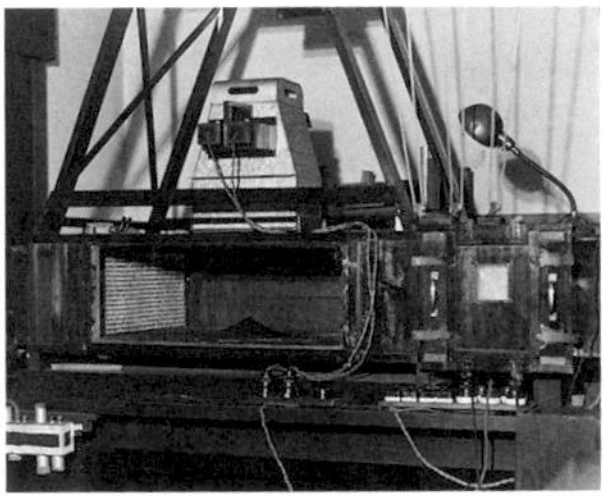

In the course of his research, Abe constructed different wind tunnel models. With various extensions, he tried to imitate the complexity of the atmosphere in the model. Using dry ice, he produced a cold current; with a lamp he simulated warming solar radiation; with a second fan he created an additional current in the tunnel. But the price of these experimental extensions was that the simulated conditions were not calculable as in the wind tunnels of the aircraft industry – the experiments merely gave Abe ideas about what the real conditions might be like.

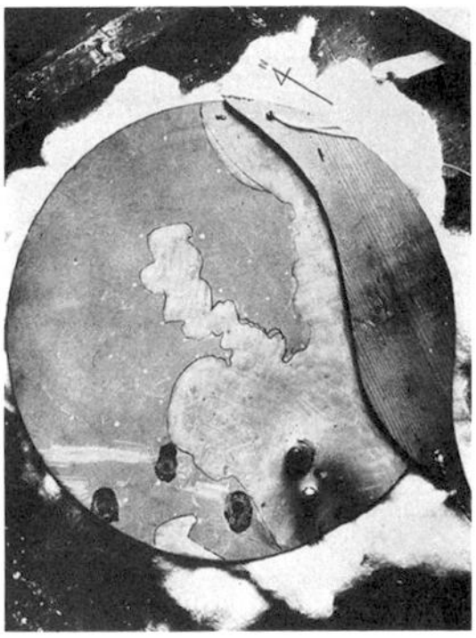

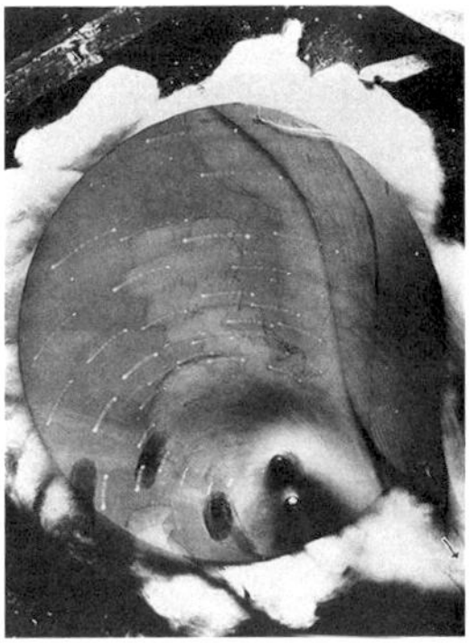

Where did Abe get the inspiration and techniques for his work? The pictures show an experiment conducted by Sakuhei Fujiwhara and Takeo Takayama in 1929. The scientists subjected a wooden board to vibrations similar to the tremors of a landscape during an earthquake. As with Abe's wind tunnel experiments, this could not be used for calculations, but was rather a playful attempt to gather ideas. In addition, in an article dating from 1921 Fujiwhara had published photographs and drawings of clouds whose shapes suggested vortexes in the air – very similar to Abe's observations in August 1926. Abe and Fujiwhara knew one another and exchanged ideas about their work.

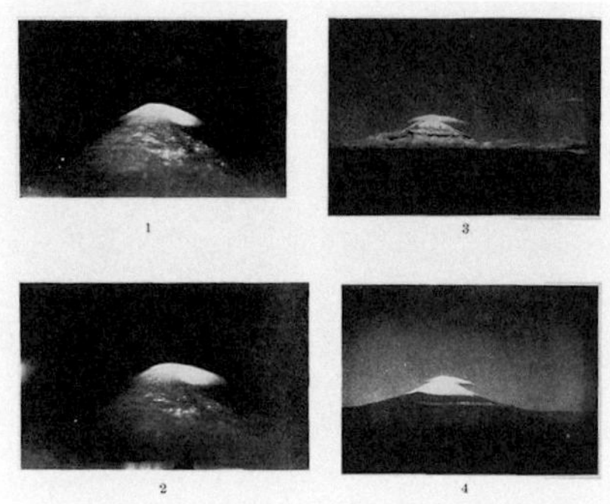

In these two image pairs published in 1932, Abe compares shots from the wind tunnel and photographs of the real mountain. In his wind tunnel, he managed to simulate a cloud cap that looks very similar to a real cloud cap above Fuji. In spite of this and similar visually convincing representations, even after years of research work Abe was not able to develop a comprehensive theory of how the air currents at the mountain are related to the shapes and movements of clouds. He could only successfully interpret special, isolated cloud movements; he was for example able to determine local wind currents within the cloud, particularly from the movement of cloud particles.

In 1941, Abe completed his research with his doctoral dissertation *Mountain Clouds, their Form and Connected Air Current*. In it, he collected the knowledge he had gained and, among other things, came up with a classification of mountain clouds, but still without an overriding theory.

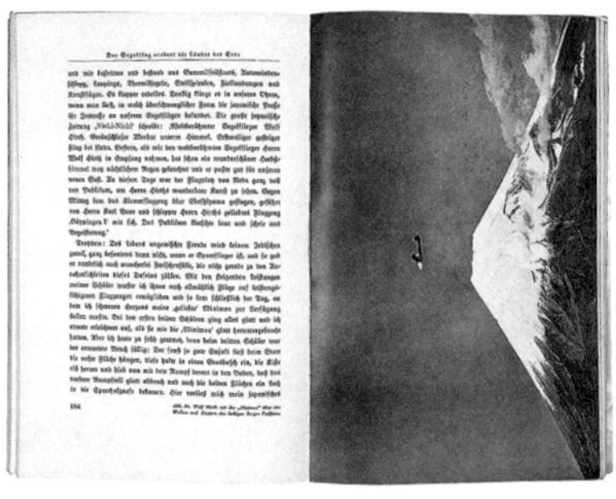

This picture was taken from the German book *Segelflug erobert die Welt* (Gliding is Conquering the World) by Georg Brütting published in 1940. Sitting in the small aircraft above Fuji is the German glider pilot

Wolf Hirth, who visited Japan in 1935. Hirth was the flight instructor of the physicist and meteorologist Joachim Küttner, who was an avid glider pilot and, like Abe, investigated the phenomenon of the special shapes of clouds at mountains. In 1938 and 1939, Küttner published two scientific works that explained the phenomenon of lee waves behind mountains. Lee waves are oscillations of airstreams that can occur when airstreams cross mountains, and can produce very specific winds and clouds. This atmospheric process, which still today is counted among the most important aspects of the behaviour of airstreams at mountains, had eluded Abe. Küttner had not viewed the mountain only at a distance, like Abe, but had gone straight into the area with his glider, experiencing the up and down of the wind on his own body.

English translation by Burke Barrett

References

Abe, Masanao, 1927,「気流の渦に生じた廻り雲の活動写真による研究」(Rotary Cloud Showing Its Figure Change)' in『気象集誌』*(Journal of the Meteorological Society of Japan 2nd ser.)* 5(7): 149–160 = Abe, Masanao, 1926–1928, 'Cinematographic Studies of Rotary Motion of a Cloud Mass near Mount Fuji' in *Geophysical Magazine* 1(5): 211–231.

Abe, Masanao, 1932, '「富士山の吊るし雲に就て」(A Peculiar Lenticular Cloud, 'Tsurushi')' in『気象集誌』*(Journal of the Meteorological Society of Japan 2nd ser.)* 10(1): 19–25 = Abe, Masanao, 1932, 'The Formation of Cloud by the Obstruction of Mt. Fuji' in *Geophysical Magazine* 6: 1–13.

Abe, Masanao, 1937, *Distribution and Movement of Cloud around Mt. Fuji Studied through Photographs at the Abe Cloud and Air Current Research Observatory, Gotemba, near Mt. Fuji, July 1932 to August 1933.* Tokyo: Central Meteorological Observatory.

Abe, Masanao, 1941,「山雲の形と気流」(*Mountain Clouds, Their Forms and Connected Air Current*). PhD thesis. Tokyo Imperial University.

Brütting, Georg, 1940, *Segelflug erobert die Welt.* Munich: Knorr & Wirth.

Küttner, Joachim, 1938, 'Moazagotl und Föhnwelle' in *Beiträge zur Physik der freien Atmosphäre* 25: 79–114.

Küttner, Joachim, 1939, *Zur Entstehung der Föhnwelle: Untersuchung auf Grund von Wellensegelflügen und Beobachtungen an der Moazagotl-Wolke.* PhD thesis. Hansische Universität zu Hamburg.

Fujiwhara, Sakuhei, and Takeo, Takayama, 1929, 'On the Mechanism of the Great Sagami Bay Earthquake on September 1, 1923' in *Bulletin of the Earthquake Research Institute* 6: 149–176.

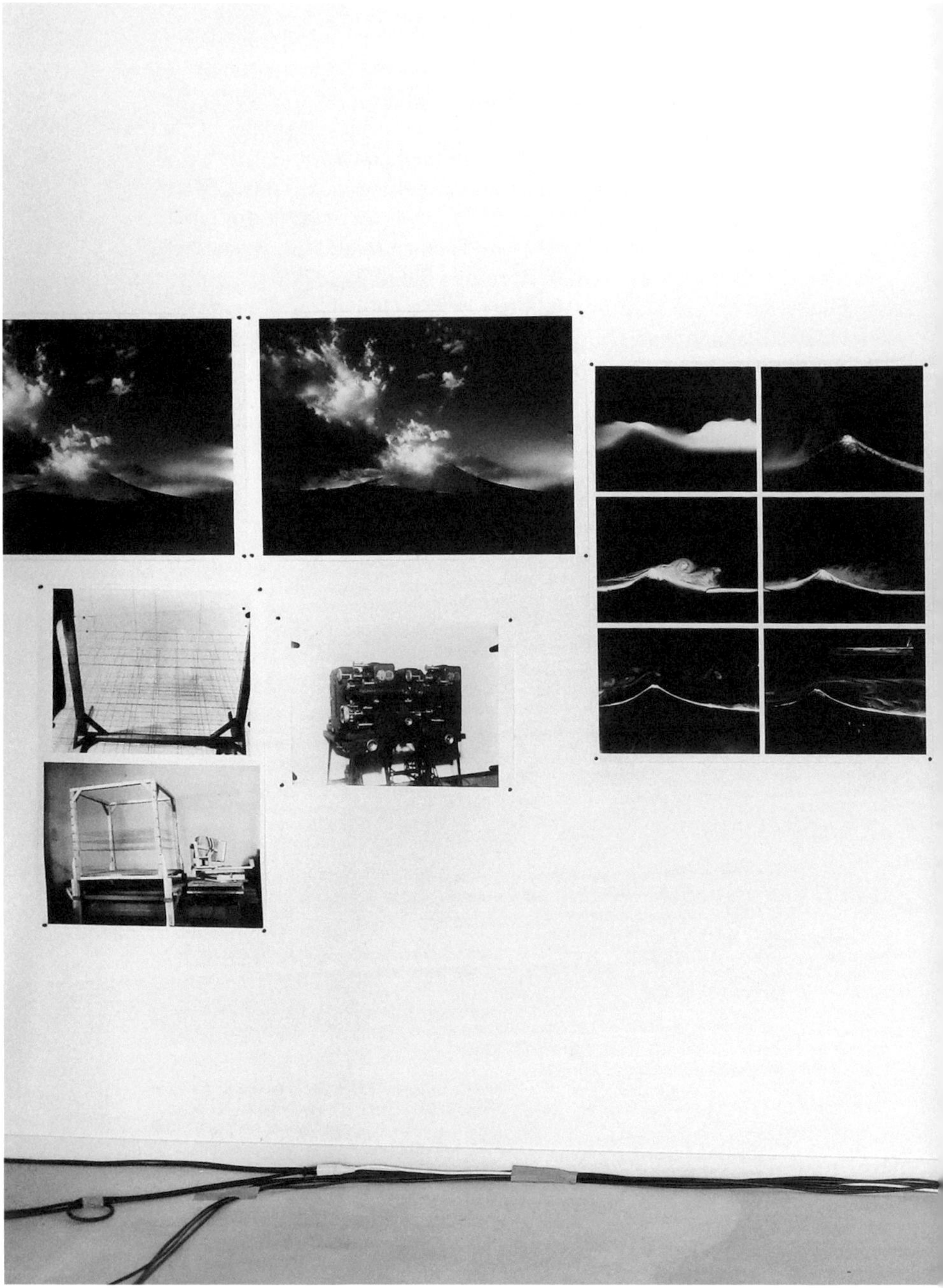

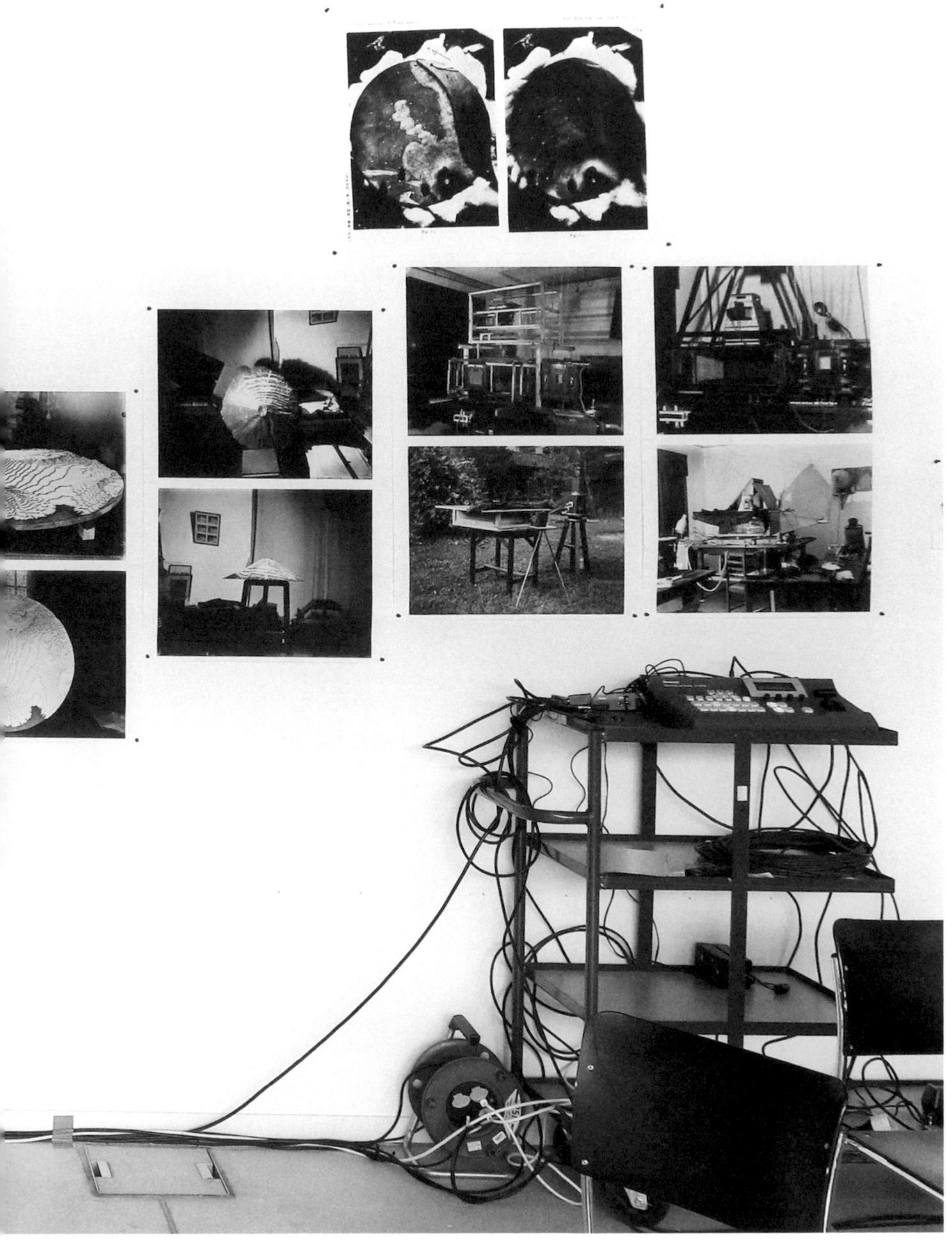

Helmut Völter (*1978, Berlin) is an artist and graphic designer. His research project *The Movement of the Clouds around Mt. Fuji* on the Japanese scientist and photographer Masanao Abe was published by Spector Books and shown at the Izu Photo Museum in Mishima, Japan.
In 2016, Völter was artist in residence at the Victoria & Albert Museum in London.

Reinhard Wendler

Orders of Magnitude in Scaling Effects

Reinhard Wendler

Orders of Magnitude in Scaling Effects

The following contribution is an attempt to correlate a number of causes, elements and theories of scaling effects, as well as solution approaches to them. So far, it has been impossible to investigate scaling processes in the form of a bigger picture because, first of all, they can be found in nearly all scientific and artistic disciplines; and second, because they are treated in various epistemic and pragmatic contexts in different, mostly oversimplified ways. Thus scaling effects are almost always understood as *problems* of measurement or scaling. As a result, dealings with them are characterized by an interest in avoiding or eliminating them, but not in analysing them thoroughly. However, since the strategies for solving the scaling effect problem belong to the multifactorial field of scaling effects itself, they are part of the bigger picture and therefore their genesis, role and impact have to be determined.

Scaling effects can be observed, among other things, in model relationships; in the change of importance or meanings or growth of organisms and organisations, databases, cities, and so on; when approaching an object or moving away from it; in the change of the speed of movement relative to an object or a landscape; in visual distortion through lenses and curved mirrors; in the vertical transfer of the observer's standpoint towards the bird's-eye or worm's-eye perspective; in the confrontation of an expectation with the actual state of affairs, etc. Various authors see the causes of scaling effects as lying in the interplay between continuous and discontinuous shifts in the above-mentioned forms of enlargements, reductions and comparisons (e.g. Galilei 1855: 124 and passim; Valéry 1970: 94 or Constantinos et al. 1972: 240). The resulting complex dynamics can manifest themselves in sporadic distortions, in value reversals, changes of meaning, importance or identity, and numerous other, often unexpected phenomena. The mathematical, physical, psychological, aesthetic and symbolic dimensions involved in these tectonics are interconnected and have an impact on one another where such shifts occur in non-uniform ways. For example, if the body of a living thing grew while its inner proportions remained the same, it would not become stronger and stronger, but weaker and weaker, finally collapsing under its own weight. Scaling effects can be observed in almost all subjects and are therefore essentially interdisciplinary objects of research. In the phenomena of scaling effects, the intertwining of disciplines and dimensions characteristic of the object in question become visible and investigable to a certain extent.

Scaling limits and orders of magnitude

In connection with scaling effects the term *scaling limits* is often used. Thus a wooden beam of a certain size can break under its own weight (Galilei 1855: 118f.), only organisms up to a certain size can live without lungs (Haldane 1928), and surveys are only meaningful with a certain minimum number of respondents. On both sides of these limits, the problem-solving methods may be different. But where exactly are the frontiers between methods? How is it possible to switch smoothly from one method to the next? Which methods should be used in each case? And – this is perhaps the question that poses itself most pressingly – what happens at the frontiers of methods, at the limits of scale themselves? With wind tunnels, the speed of sound is such a scale limit at which a methodological change would be needed. In wind tunnels with wind speeds lower or higher than the speed of sound, relatively continuous conditions prevail. In transonic wind tunnels, in which the wind blows at about sonic speed, numerous phenomena occur that cannot be observed in the other two cases. Based on these phenomena, it is not only apparent that there are discontinuities at the boundaries between one scale and another. Additionally, researchers are inundated cornucopia-like by phenomena that are difficult or impossible to get under control. Transonic wind tunnels lie, so to speak, at the aerodynamic scaling limit of about 1235 kilometres an hour. The challenges a theoretical investigation of the processes and phenomena faces provide a good example of the mercurialness of scaling limits. Vitruvius' observation based on ancient architecture that not everything can be carried out using the same methods outlines a problem area that comes up in twentieth-century wind tunnel technology as well as in many other disciplines. The need for *three* general types of wind tunnels makes it clear that at scaling limits often one method cannot be directly replaced by another, but in many cases a third is needed by means of which the scaling limits can be leapfrogged.

At scaling limits, scaling effects occur that are considered relevant in the context in question. One can envision scaling limits as corridors which are formed by scaling effects and run through the phenomenal domain in question. On both sides of these no-man's lands, scaling effects are rarer or do not affect the actions of the planners, designers or researchers. Continuous fields between scaling limits are often called *orders of magnitude*. An example of an encounter with a scaling limit is Saint Pierre cathedral in Beauvais, which partially collapsed twice and today has to be secured with an elaborate system of scaffoldings, belts and monitoring systems.[1] In its current condition, the building's statics are still dangerously close to the scaling limit. The closer they come to it, the more numerous and various the measures have to be to secure the

1 Cf. Wind Tunnel Bulletin (2014: 22–23); see also Murray (1997) and Mark (1982: 58–77).

building. If the scaling limit is surpassed, the available safeguards are no longer sufficient and the building collapses. An increase in the distance to the static scaling limits entails a decrease in the number and heterogeneity of the required statics-related measures. Thus the second partial collapse of Beauvais Cathedral in 1573 was preceded by the erection of a tower on the unstable nave. Because of the tower, the static scaling limit was exceeded. There was no time to take protective measures on account of the abrupt process.

Many scaling effects depend in various ways on one's conception of the object, in other words, on what the reference object is viewed as, and in what way (Mahr 2010). This can be observed with scale models in the sciences, for example. The use of measurement data that can be obtained based on the model usually cannot be transferred unchanged to the object to which they are to be applied. As Max Black writes:

> Sheer change of size may upset the balance of factors in the original. Too small a model of a uranium bomb will fail to explode, too large a reproduction of a housefly will never get off the ground, and the solar system cannot be expected to look like its planetarium model. Inferences from scale model to original are intrinsically precarious and in need of supplementary validation and correction. (2011: 256)

In such cases the term *scaling effects* is often used. However, there is no *physical* relationship between the model and the object to which it is to be applied, such as e.g. a relationship of growth, but only a *conceived one*. The scaling effects therefore also depend on the conception. They result from the notion of continuous growth of the model and discontinuous changes that take place at the same time. While one could arguably build and measure a large number of models in different intermediate sizes in order to identify these discontinuous changes in more detail, furnishing such proof is considered superfluous and thus dispensed with. Furthermore, the coexistence of continuous and discontinuous changes of an object does not lead to appreciable scaling effects in every case. They are only consciously perceived when tolerance limits are exceeded – for example, in the case of Beauvais Cathedral.

Scaling effects like these are problems that stand in the way of a given planning, design or knowledge goal. In such cases, the scaling effect in question is addressed deliberately. If the relevant problems recur, often methods are developed to prevent them from having negative influences, or to reduce their negative impact on the process. Thus a comprehensive pool of formulas was developed to be applied in scale models used in aerodynamics; with the help of these formulas the measurement result can be transferred from the model to the object to which it is to be applied despite the scaling limits lying between them (Waltenspül 2015). Many architects claim to be able to assess a projected building based on a scale model and thus to transfer the model via a number of scaling limits, as it were, and to imagine it as a completed building. Architects complain that very few laypeople, customers or committees confronted with the model have this ability. As a result, they say, very beautifully elaborated models can be used to serve as window dressing. "My complaint [...] is that the clients look at the model, and nobody studies it, and the architects sell the job, good or bad. Sometimes I think we've gotten worse architecture along with this wonderful tool" (Theodore Conrad quoted from Lebensohn 1988: 35; also cf. Moon 2005: 114).

Aside from such scaling effects that manifest themselves in the form of problems, there are others that are only noticeable when attention is focused on them explicitly. For example, if one approaches a building from a great distance until one is standing directly at its wall, the visual appearance of the structure runs through a number of different qualities. From a certain proximity, for example, one no longer has a view of the whole structure, while other aspects not considered until then capture attention. Although such changes, and many others, in the visual appearance of the edifice occur, they are marginalised by the conceptual notion of the continuity of the building and the perception thereof (see e.g. Latour Yaneva 2008). Most of the scaling effects pass unnoticed because they do not occur as problems. They can be removed from their marginalisation if one focuses one's attention on them and thus makes them visible again. Ultimately, scaling effects can be found everywhere if one only looks for them.

Scaling limits and disciplines

The beginnings of the history of reflexion on scaling effects must be considerably older than the oldest preserved written documents. As the ancient Greeks' books on architecture have been lost, the oldest preserved written reference to scaling effects presumably stems from Vitruvius. In the Tenth Book of his treatise on architecture, we read in chapter 16:

> For not all things are practicable on identical principles, but there are some things which, when enlarged in imitation of small models, are effective, others can not have models, but are constructed independently of them, while there are some which appear feasible in models, but when they have begun to increase in size are impracticable ... (1914: 316)

Vitruvius differentiates between *three* relationships: First, those in which *no* scaling effects occur; second, those which do not admit any *reduction* beyond a certain degree; and third, those that do not admit any *enlargement*. Thus Vitruvius implicitly distinguishes between scale invariance, scaling effects with a decrease in size, and scaling effects with an increase in size, which suggests he had extensive practical and theoretical knowledge of scaling effects.

A milestone in scientific investigation of scaling effects is Galileo's work *Discourses and Mathematical Demonstrations*

Relating to Two New Sciences from 1638. Among other things, the book deals with the fact discussed in mechanics ever since that load-bearing structures can collapse under their own weight if they reach a certain size. Galileo speaks of the "inobbedienza delle macchine in concreto alle medesime astratte e ideali" (1855: 3),[2] or the "deviations disobedience observed between of the concrete machines in the concrete and into the abstract" (Galilei 2010: 51). The ideal machine is continuous, as it were, while the physical one is subject to a number of discontinuous conditions. Galileo suggests that the physical machine is disobedient vis-à-vis our plans and ideas. The *Discourses and Mathematical Demonstrations Relating to Two New Sciences* not only have eminent importance for the history of mechanics, but also for the history of theoretical confrontation with scaling limits and scaling effects.

With Galileo's dialogue, scaling effects become palpable as a reference object. They are predicted with mathematical means, and as a result their static challenges can be met differently. Eugène Viollet-le-Duc, for example, speaks of the relation of materials to scale, in other words the scale that the material imposes on the architect (cf. Boudon 2003: 106). And D'Arcy Thompson writes: "Gravitation not only limits the magnitude but controls the form of things" (1945: 67). Different building materials have different scaling limits and thus influence the link between scaling effects and building forms. Due to the rise of steel in the nineteenth century, for instance, scaling limits could be pushed to new limits and thus new orders of magnitude and building forms developed. The Eiffel Tower is perhaps the most well-known structure reflecting this shift (see e.g. Grigsby 2012).

Beginning with architecture and the engineering sciences, the idea of scaling limits and scaling effects was extended to social theory, initially by Robert Thomas Malthus in

2 See also Kurrer (1989 & 1992) and Freddi (2014).

his *Essay on the Principle of Population* (1798). It has since recurred in different forms, for example in the study "The Limits to Growth" first presented in St. Gallen (Meadows et al. 1972). At the end of the nineteenth century, the idea was influenced by evolutionary theory in biology, leading to contributions such as Haldane's *On Being the Right Size* (1926), D'Arcy Thompson's *On Growth and Form* (1945), and recently Chris McGowan's *Diatoms to Dinosaurs: The Size and Scale of Living Things* (1994). The scaling issue has also played a key role in the arts since the mid nineteenth century. Many works of avant-garde artists, for example, reflect the series of accelerations that were caused by steam engines, steamships, locomotives, telegraphy, the automobile, the airplane, and so on. Futurism was one of the avant-garde art movements whose works and manifestos reflect this investigation most clearly. In the 1960s, György Kepes identified a "crisis of scale" (Kepes 1960: 7) between the rapid acceleration of the world and the related shrinking of space on the one hand, and the still existent pre- and early industrial visual models on the other (Virilio 1978). He attempted to counter this scaling crisis with new art forms that managed to make the "new scales" (Kepes 1969: iv) palpable.

Scaling and scaling limits have not only been taken up in more and more fields, but have also led to the formation of new disciplines. These often start with reports about liminal experiences at the threshold to a new, hitherto unknown order of magnitude. In Galileo's dialogue Sagredo says: "My brain already reels. My mind, like a cloud momentarily illuminated by a lightning-flash, is for an instant filled with an unusual light, which now beckons to me and which now suddenly mingles and obscures strange, crude ideas" (Galilei 2010: 51; original in Italian).[3] D'Arcy Thompson writes in *On Growth and Form* about the order of magnitude of microbiology:

3 Original Italian text: "Io già mi sento rivolgere il cervello, e, quasi nugola dal baleno repentinamente aperta, ingombrarmisi la mente da momentanea ed insolita luce, che da lontano mi accenna e subito confonde ed asconde immaginazioni straniere ed indigeste" (Galilei 1855: 7).

"[W]e have come to the edge of a world of which we have no experience, and where all our preconceptions must be recast" (1945: 77). Regarding literary and poetic examinations of the world of small things, Gaston Bachelard notes: "You have to dispense with logic in order to experience the big within the small" (1978: 124). According to Pietro Bellasi, "the interweaving of the *smallest* and *largest* creates a complex metaphorical image of a reality perceived as a distant and threatening differentness" (1985: 229–230, original in French).

Since Galileo, efforts to go beyond these horizons and examine the worlds that lie behind them have repeatedly led to the formation of new disciplines. Examples include continuum mechanics, population theory and architecturology. Thus, for example, the architecture theoretician Philippe Boudon raised the issue of scaling (échelle) to the level of a paradigm of a novel architecturology (1991b & 2002). Scaling limits, between which planners mediate and which they have to try to bring into an overarching system, play an essential role in this theory. One cannot, Boudon writes, always use only one measuring tape, for it "cannot be stretched [...] without tearing it. In that event, there is thus a cut, a change of space, a change of scale" (2003: 106, original in French). The same applies to scientific measuring systems that are appropriate for their objects and scale limits. A zeptometer,[4] a foot, a light year[5] and a parsec[6] are not only used to avoid long series of zeros, but also because such means can be employed to encompass *orders of magnitude* which have their own logics, as it were. The identification of new orders of magnitude is often coupled with the formation of new fields of research and career profiles which despite having the same ground of being, usually have little contact with one another.

In the last few decades the large number of relevant scales has become more and more of an issue, be it through

4 A three-billionth of a metre.
5 9.461 trillion kilometres.
6 30.86 billion kilometres.

so-called multiscale approaches (cf. Fish 2010, Sih 2007, Barth et al. 2002, Engquist et al. 2009, and Borja 2011), by means of which the transfer from one order of magnitude to another can be achieved, or through overview-like compilations, including those of D'Arcy Thompson (1945: 66), Kees Boeke (1957), Philip and Phylis Morrison (1982), Philippe Boudon (2002), José Carlos Del Toro Iniesta et al. (2006) or of Gerard 't Hooft and Stefan Vandoren (2014). In the twentieth century, a new standard of scale was established with powers of ten. D'Arcy Thompson commented on this as follows:

> It is a remarkable thing, worth pausing to reflect on, that we can pass so easily and in a dozen lines from molecular magnitudes to the dimensions of a Sequoia or a whale. Addition and subtraction, the old arith metic of the Egyptians, are not powerful enough for such an operation; but the story of the grains of wheat upon the chessboard shewed the way, and Archimedes and Napier elaborated the arithmetic of multiplication. So passing up and down by easy steps, as Archimedes did when he numbered the sands of the sea, we compare the magnitudes of the great beasts and the small, of the atoms of which they are made, and the world in which they dwell. (1945: 66–67)

Here not only living things, but also orders of magnitude become comparable to each other, and they can even be transferred to a new scale. The measuring marks on this scale are formed by powers of ten, on the one hand, and by the scaling limits and the scaling effects occurring at them on the other. The scale of scales belongs to a long series of related attempts to find a more general term for the heterogeneity caused by scale limits and scaling effects and thus enable them to be examined. In an interview on the television channel 3Sat, Claus Pias emphasised that due to their ubiquity scaling problems enable a problem-oriented exchange between all kinds of disciplines.[7] Thus scaling effects can be transformed from a problem into an advantage.

Scaling theory as proto-discipline

The expression *scaling effect* plays an important role in such attempts at establishing all-encompassing perspectives for investigation. It is ahead of the examination of the phenomena named after it because its conciseness and handiness suggest a concise and handy object of investigation. In the sense of "epistemic ballistics" (Wendler 2013), it creates an aporia in the field of tension between scaling and effect, which calls for new ways of thinking. It generates an unanswered question to which it simultaneously refers like a signpost or tombstone. Numerous objects, phenomena, observations and perspectives can be interrelated at this reference point, which is perceived to be palpable and continuous. The term *scaling effect*, as well as some of the phenomena designated by it, is able to conjure up a location, to bring local configurations and experimental systems into exchange by means of questions, problems and solution strategies and thus to establish a partly latent, partly actual network. In this form, it generates a kind of proto-discipline, a field of research that has only been partly institutionalized and has only partly made its way to the consciousness of the actors involved (Wendler 2013). This research field depends directly on what its protagonists actually do, whether and what they publish or whether and how they include or exclude those belonging to other disciplines.

In most cases, the encounter with scaling effects occurs in the problem-solving mode, which also means that it occurs in a hermetic way, as it were. The problem is resolved or bypassed depending on the situation, and the methods that prove to be helpful achieve the status of a locally valid routine.

7 Cf. Pias, Claus, with Gerd Scobel in the science TV programme *Scobel* on 3Sat, 16 September 2010.

Owing to the link of the solutions to concrete, quasi local settings, the different approaches are only rarely compared with each other. As long as the problem can be solved or bypassed, a generalisation is not necessary. Thus, in many cases only potential solutions for processes that are interlinked anyway come into contact with one another. Cross-situational, or even cross-disciplinary, comparisons of possible solutions are rare; usually they are only needed when the problems cannot be solved or circumvented and therefore research in other fields seems sensible. However, a comprehensive comparison of different potential solutions does not lead to a more general theory of scaling, but to a more general theory on how to solve scaling problems. Confusing problem-solving strategies with a theory of the problem engenders philosophical monsters.

Problem-solving strategies that are used as problem descriptions often claim validity in natural and engineering science as well as philosophy. They effectively hinder a confrontation with the incalculability and heterogeneity of the object under investigation. The *solution* to the problem is still in the foreground; a bypassing or undefining, as it were, of aspects that inhibit, elude, or thwart fluid speech. For this reason, the research on scaling effects exhibits characteristics of archaeological excavation work. The digging area is still largely untouched and invites archaeologists to explore it. Substantial finds wait under a layer of more or less relevant theories to be discovered and demystified. Seen in this way, the movement out of the field of obsolete concepts compiled from pragmatic ad-hoc solutions occurs as a decisive orientation to the problems themselves, the scaling effects, and scaling limits. György Kepes called for and promoted this kind of orientation back in 1969 when he wrote: "We may suffer from the new scale, but we have to go forward and meet it" (1969: iv). Kepes related this to the menacing new world of intercontinental missiles, satellites and telecommunications technologies. But his plea can also be linked to the dimensions of scaling itself.

It is not the question of how to get rid of the problem as fast and completely as possible that leads to the goal, but the question of how all the factors involved interact with each other and which phenomena result.

English translation by Burke Barrett

References

Bachelard, Gaston, 1978, *Poétique de l'Espace*. Paris: PUF.

Barth, Timothy. J. et al. (eds.), 2002, *Multiscale and Multiresolution Methods: Theory and Applications*. Berlin: Springer.

Bellasi, Pietro, 1985, 'Lilliput et Brobdingnag: Métaphores de l'imaginaire miniaturisant et mégalisant' in *Communications* 42(1): 229–244.

Black, Max, 2011, 'Models and Archetypes' in Gimbel, Steven, *Exploring the Scientific Method: Cases and Questions*. Chicago: University Of Chicago Press: 256–264.

Boeke, Kees, 1957, *Cosmic View: The Universe in 40 Jumps*. New York: John Day Corp.

Bony, Jean, 1983, *French Gothic Architecture of the 12th and 13th Centuries*. Berkeley: University of California Press.

Borja, Ronaldo I. (ed.), 2011, *Multiscale and Multiphysics Processes in Geomechanics: Results of the Workshop on Multiscale and Multiphysics Processes in Geomechanics*, Stanford, June 2010. Heidelberg: Springer.

Boudon, Philippe, 1991a, *Der architektonische Raum: Über das Verhältnis von Bauen und Erkennen* (trans. Marianne Uhl). Basel: Birkhäuser Verlag.

Boudon, Philippe (ed.), 1991b, *De l'architecture à l'épistémologie: La question de l'échelle*. Paris: PUF.

Boudon, Philippe, 2002, *Échelle(s): L'architecture comme travail de l'épistémologue*. Paris: Economica.

Boudon, Philippe, 2003, *Sur l'espace architectural: essai d'épistémologie de l'architecture*. Marseille: Parenthèses.

Como, Mario, 2009, 'The Collapse of the Beauvais Cathedral in 1284: The Conjecture of the Creep Buckling Piers' in *Proceedings of the Third International Congress on Construction History 1*, Berlin: NEUNPLUS1: 393–400.

Del Toro Iniesta, José Carlos et al., 2006, *The Many Scales in the Universe. JENAM 2004 Astrophysics Reviews*. Dordrecht: Springer.

Doxiadis, Constantinos et al. (Delos Seven), 1972, 'The Scale of Settlements and the Quality of Life' in Bell, Gwen, and Jacqueline Tyrwhitt (eds.), *Human Identity in the Urban Environment*. Harmondsworth: Penguin.

Engquist, Björn, et al. (eds.), 2009, *Multiscale Modeling and Simulation in Science*. Berlin: Springer.

Fish, Jacob (ed.), 2010, *Multiscale Methods: Bridging the Scales in Science and Engineering*. New York: Oxford University Press.

Freddi, Antonio, 2014, 'L'effetto scala, il vuoto e i diversi infiniti nella prima giornata dei "Discorsi intorno a due nuove scienze" di Galileo Galilei' in *Kínesis* 6(11): 165–186.

Galilei, Galileo, 1855, 'Discorsi e dimostrazioni matematiche intorno a due nuove scienze attenenti alla meccanica ed ai movimenti locali', in *Le opere di Galileo Galilei: Prima edizione completa, Vol. XIII.* Florence: Societa Editrice Fiorentina (1634).

Galiei, Galileo, 2010, *Dialogues Concerning Two New Sciences* (trans. H. Crew, A. de Salvio). New York: Cosimo Classics (1914).

Grigsby, Darcy Grimaldo, 2012, *Colossal: Engineering Modernity – Suez Canal, Statue of Liberty, Eiffel Tower, and Panama Canal.* Pittsburgh: Periscope.

Haldane, John Burdon Sanderson, 1928, 'On Being the Right Size' in *Possible Worlds: and Other Essays.* London: Chatoo and Windus: 18–44.

Kepes, György, 1960, 'Introduction to the Issue, The Visual Arts Today' in *Daedalus* 89(1, Winter): 3–12.

Kepes, György, 1969, *Language of Vision: Painting, Photography, Advertising-Design.* Chicago: Paul Theobold.

Kurrer, Karl-Eugen, 1989, 'Die Anfänge der Festigkeitslehre in Galileo Galileis "Discorsi"' in *Humanismus und Technik, Jahrbuch 1988* (32): 33–61.

Kurrer, Karl-Eugen, 1992, 'Zur Frühgeschichte der Festigkeitslehre' in Scheidegger, Fritz (ed.), *Aus der Geschichte der Bautechnik, Band II.* Basel: Birkhäuser Verlag: 49–63.

Latour, Bruno, and Albena Yaneva, 2008, 'Give Me a Gun and I Will Make All Buildings Move. An ANT´s View of Architecture' in Geiser, Reto (ed.), *Explorations in Architecture: Teaching, Design, Research.* Basel: Birkhäuser Verlag: 80–89.

Lebensohn, Jeremy, 1988, 'Mighty Miniatures' in *American Craft* 48(3): 34–39.

McGowan, Chris, 1994, *Diatoms to Dinosaurs: The Size and Scale of Living Things.* Washington: Island Books.

Mahr, Bernd, 2010, 'Intentionality and Modelling of Conception' in Bab, Sebastian, and Klaus Robering, *Judgements and Propositions: Logical, Linguistic, and Cognitive Issues.* Berlin: Logos Verlag: 61–87.

Malthus, Robert Thomas, 1798, *Essay on the Principle of Population.* London: Johnson.

Manner, Robert, 1962, 'Le Maître de la cathédrale de Beauvais' in *Art de France* 2: 77–92.

Mark, Robert, 1982, *Experiments in Gothic Structure.* Cambridge: MIT Press.

Meadows, Donella H., et al., 1972, *The Limits to Growth: A Report for the Club of Rome's Project on the Predicament of Mankind.* New York: Universe Books.

Morrison, Philip, and Phylis Morrison, 1982, *Powers of Ten: About the Relative Size of Things in the Universe.* New York: Scientific American Library.

Moon, Karen, 2005, *Modeling Messages: The Architect and the Model.* New York: Monacelli.

Murray, Stephen, 1989, *Beauvais Cathedral: Architecture of Transcendence.* Princeton: Princeton University Press.

Murray, Stephen, 1997, 'The Collapse of 1284 at Beauvais Cathedral' in Courtenay, Lynn T. (ed.) *The Engineering of Medieval Cathedrals.* Brookfield, Vt.: Ashgate/Variorum: 141–168.

Sih, George C. (ed.), 2007, *Multiscaling in Molecular Continuum Mechanics: Interaction of Time and Size from Macro to Nano.* Berlin: Springer.

'T Hooft, Gerard, and Stefan Vandoren, 2014, *Time in Powers of Ten: Natural Phenomena and Their Timescales.* Singapore: World Scientific Publishing Company.

Thompson, D'Arcy Wentworth, 1945, *On Growth and Form.* Cambridge University Press.

Valéry, Paul, 1970, *Eupalinos ou l´architecte – L'Âme et la Danse – Dialogue de l'Arbre.* Paris: Gallimard.

Viollet-le-Duc, Eugène, 1858, *Dictionnaire raisonné de l'architecture française du XIe au XVIe siècle* Vol I. Paris: Morel.

Virilio, Paul, 1978, *Fahren, fahren, fahren...* (trans. U. Rauff). Berlin: Merve Verlag.

Vitruvius, 1914, *The Ten Books on Architecture* (trans. M. H. Morgan). London: Oxford University Press.

Waltenspül, Sarine, 2015, 'Der Kosmos aus der Petrischale. Oder: Wie lässt das Ähnlichkeitsprinzip Universen entstehen?' in Jürgens, Anna-Sophie, and Tassilo Tesche (eds.), *LaborARTorium: Forschung im Denkraum zwischen Wissenschaft und Kunst. Eine Methodenreflexion.* Bielefeld: Transcript Verlag: 109–121.

Wendler, Reinhard, 2013, 'Epistemische Ballistik und die Rhetorik der Unverhältnismässigkeit' in Dombois, Florian, et al., *Präparat Bergsturz. Vol 2.* Luzern: Periferia: 57–67.

Wind Tunnel Bulletin #2. The Scale Effect. 2014 (June). Zurich.
Online at: http://windtunnelbulletin.zhdk.ch/02/ (accessed 30 January 2017).

Reinhard Wendler is a research associate at the Max Planck Institute for Art History in Florence. He studied art history, musicology and philosophy at the TU Berlin and the Humboldt University of Berlin, where he completed his doctoral dissertation on models in work and cognitive processes in 2008. His monograph *Das Modell zwischen Kunst und Wissenschaft* (The Model Between Art and Science) was published by Fink-Verlag in 2013.

Juliet Koss

Proposal for *Model Soviets*

Juliet Koss

Proposal for *Model Soviets*

Taking as its broader context the Soviet obsession with construction in the 1920s and 1930s, *Model Soviets* explores the status and function of models (in the form of art objects, architectural designs or more abstract representations of future possibilities) in early Soviet culture. Based primarily on previously unpublished images from archives and collections in Canada, Europe and the United States, this book ranges chronologically from Vladimir Tatlin's *Model for the Monument to the Third International* of 1919–20 (perhaps the most famous model of the twentieth century) to a series of pamphlets that were distributed at the Soviet Pavilion at the New York World's Fair in 1939. It investigates the central role of models in the Soviet Union's first two decades, when Communism itself operated both as a daily practice undergoing constant reformulation and as a conceptual model for the future, and reveals how images of the architectural process, from initial designs to completed buildings, represented the formation of the Soviet state and, by extension, the model citizens of this new nation. As objects of a given size, models are intended (if sometimes only theoretically) for construction at a later moment: larger, elsewhere. They thus engage with and even embody scale and temporality, central themes in early Soviet culture that invoke the nation's geographic breadth, political authority and power. Conceptually loaded and politically charged, Soviet models revealed not only their makers' ingenuity and the creative force of their remarkable historical moment but also, more generally, the extraordinary potential of future Soviet achievements.

The proliferation of models in early Soviet culture was recorded, augmented and disseminated by a plethora of images of models, design projects and architectural and urban constructions. Documentary images, both still and moving, conveyed a crucial message in this rich and pivotal era of modern photography in the Soviet Union: playing with scale and temporality, they made designs for the future seem attainable and sometimes even suggested that completion had already – if impossibly – been achieved. If models were utopian proposals for post-Revolutionary creativity, then photographs and films of models (and, to a lesser extent, images of actual construction projects) became what might be termed 'model images'. Operating between architecture, the visual arts, science fiction and documentary imagery, models and their images presented the potential convergence or even dissolution of the traditional categories of creative production and offered not only radical accomplishments but also plausible proposals for the Soviet future.

Model Soviets eschews the traditional art-historical narrative of heroic post-Revolutionary advances followed by aesthetic failure and political compromise, instead presenting Soviet work in the 1920s and 1930s in the visual arts and architecture as a continuous reinvention of cultural practice and an ongoing engagement with that nation's cultural, economic and sociopolitical changes. It includes the work of such major figures as Boris Iofan, Kazimir Malevich, Alexander Medvedkin, Alexander

Rodchenko, Alexei Shchusev, Viktor Shklovsky, Varvara Stepanova, Vladimir Tatlin, Sergei Tret'iakov and Dziga Vertov; it also attends to countless snapshots by anonymous photographers, situating this material in relation to European modernism and the Soviet experience of modernization. Working from an interdisciplinary premise and incorporating photography, photomontage and film as well as painting, drawing, three-dimensional work, printed matter, poetry and literature,

Model Soviets focuses on representations of architectural designs, construction projects, buildings covered in scaffolding and completed edifices to argue that such imagery made expert use of visual scale, shifting temporality and an evolving documentary aesthetic to present utopian visions as monumental facts even as the Soviet nation itself remained chaotically under construction.

Chapter 1: Model Utopia

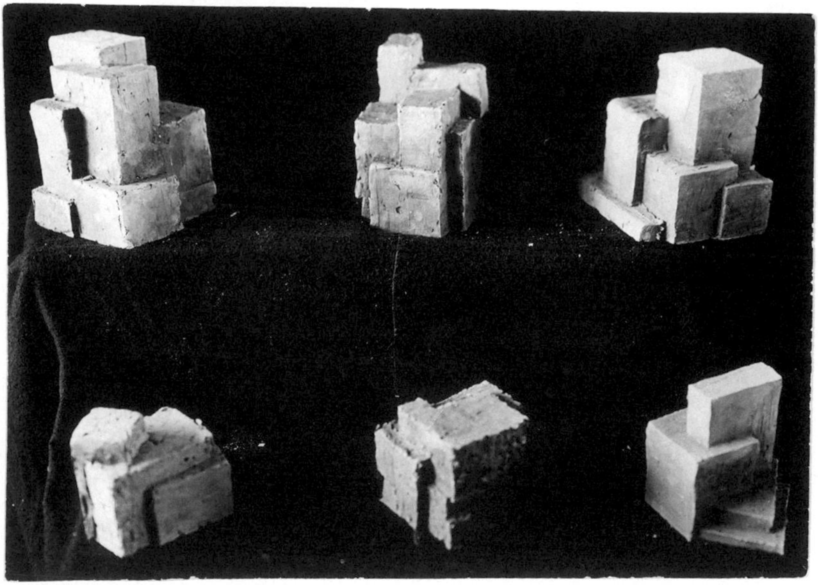

Unknown photographer. Photograph of student models on the topic "Interaction of Volumes: Plastic Construction" for the "Volume" course at the VKhUTEMAS (Higher State Artistic Technical Studios), Moscow, between 1920 and 1926. Gelatin silver print, 11.5 x 16.2 cm. Collection Centre Canadien de l'Architecture/Canadian Centre for Architecture, Montréal. Gift of Howard Schickler and David Lafaille.

Chapter 2: Monumental Snapshots

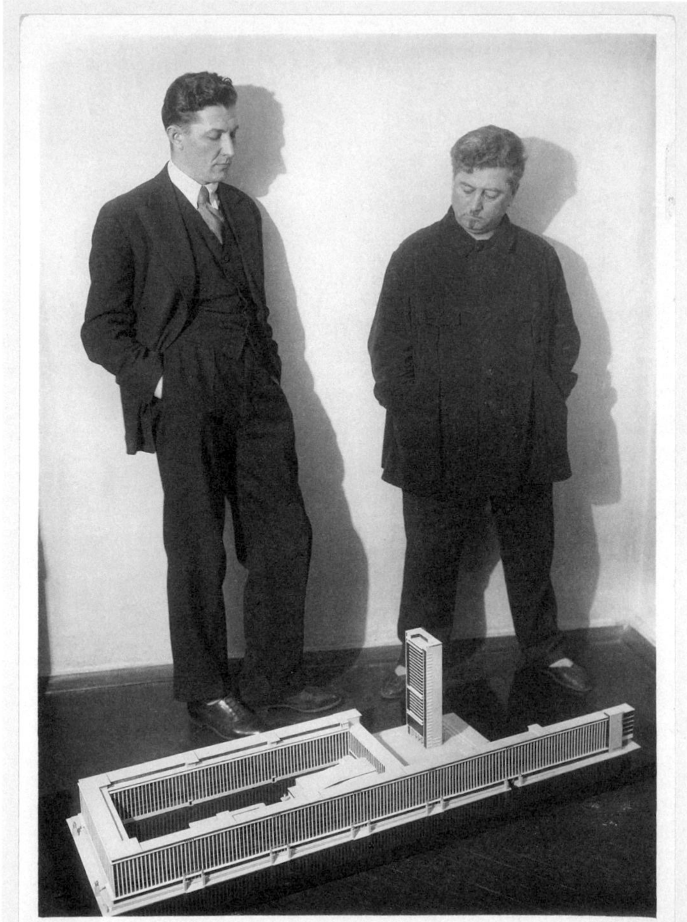

Unknown photographer. Portrait of Danil F. Fridman and Gleb Glushchenko with a model for the Building of Industry, Sverdlovsk, Soviet Union (now Ekaterinburg, Russia), 1930–1. Gelatin silver print, 22.6 x 15.9 cm. Collection Centre Canadien de l'Architecture/Canadian Centre for Architecture, Montréal.

Chapter 3: Under Construction

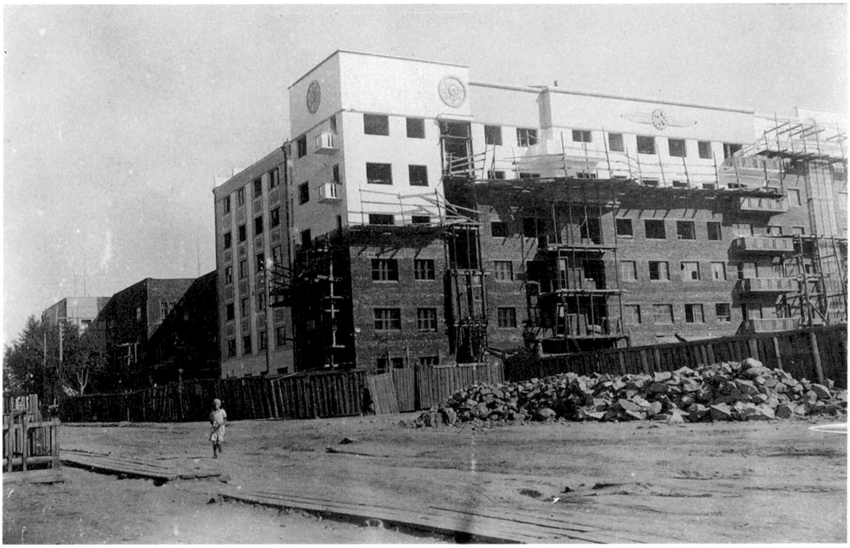

Unknown photographer. View of a government office building [?] under construction, Novosibirsk, Soviet Union. Gelatin silver print, 14.3 x 22.7 cm. Collection Centre Canadien de l'Architecture/Canadian Centre for Architecture, Montréal.

Chapter 4: Time Machines

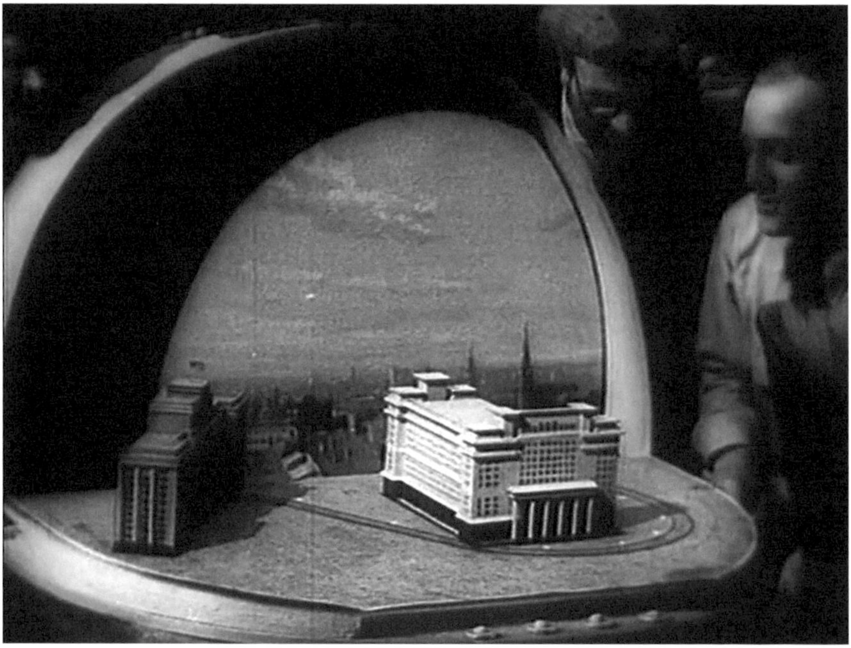

Alexander Medvedkin, film still from The New Moscow, *1938. Image courtesy of Light Industry, New York.*

Chapter 5: Happy Model Childhood

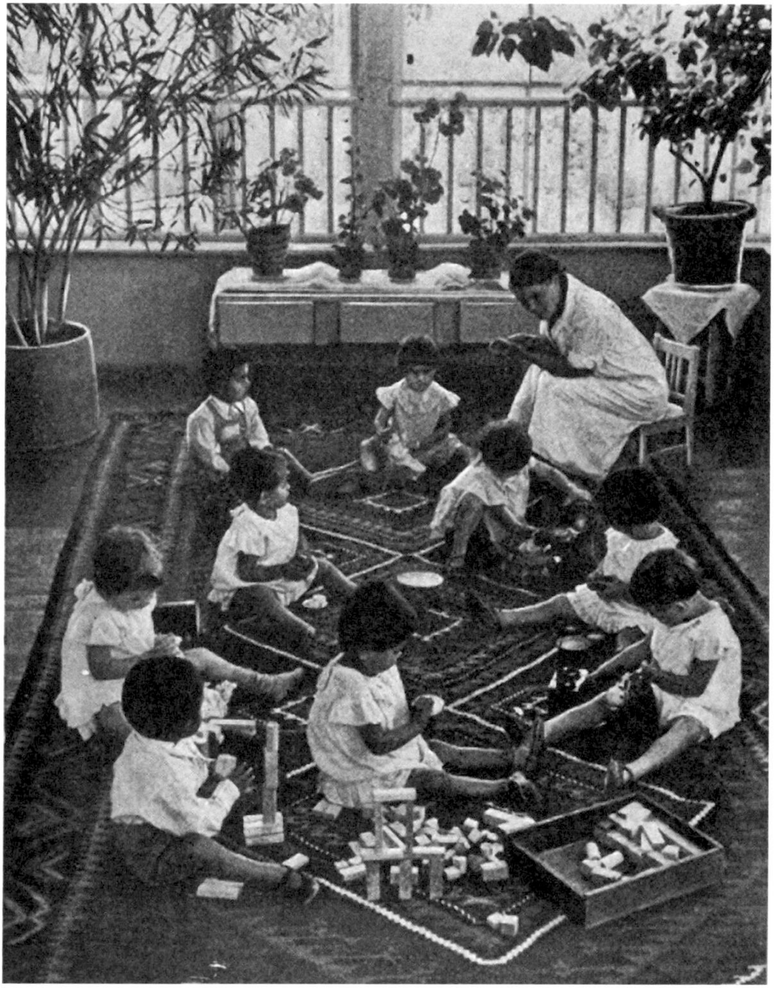

"In the nursery of the Stalin Textile Mills in Tashkent," illustration from M. Ilin, The Little Citizen of a Big Country *(Moscow: Foreign Languages Publishing House, 1939).*

Juliet Koss is a professor of art history at Scripps College in Claremont, California. A specialist in modern German and Soviet art and architecture, she is the author of *Modernism after Wagner* (University of Minnesota Press, 2010) and has held fellowships at, among others, the American Academy in Berlin, the Getty Research Institute, the Canadian Centre for Architecture, the Humboldt Foundation, the Clark Art Institute and the Harriman Institute at Columbia University.

Mirjam Steiner

Inseparably United: Big and Small in Literary Settings

Mirjam Steiner

Inseparably United: Big and Small in Literary Settings

Migraineurs know the symptoms: there is a shimmering, a tingling sensation, the visual field is reduced and suddenly everything looks small – or big. As a side effect of a migraine aura or a harbinger of an epileptic seizure, the affected persons' perception can change and they can experience their surroundings as being strongly distorted. *Micropsia* and *macropsia* are the neurological terms for the peculiar sensation of shrinking or growing. In addition, the person's sense of time can even alter. In professional medical literature this visual disorder is known as *Alice in Wonderland*

Syndrome[1], referring to the eponymous novel by the English author Lewis Carroll, who is said to have suffered from migraine himself.

Nothing but losses

The juxtaposition of big and small is anything but harmless. This is documented by neurological perceptual disorders and numerous examples from literature alike. For where there is scaling, norms are questioned and systems of order are dissolved. Losses, interruptions, dissonances, distortions, and exaggerations are the order of the day. And this is always existential!

Scaling effects are prominently represented at the level of character descriptions. In *Alice in Wonderland* (1865), the child protagonist enters a kind of dream world through an infinitely long tunnel

1 For alterations in perception in the context of a migraine attack, see Hustvedt (2012).

and, after eating cake and drinking a magic potion, opens out like a telescope and then concertinas again. Having become gigantic, she hits her head on the ceiling, is locked in a room and unable to move, and – having shrunk again – almost drowns in a sea of her own tears. What she initially supposes is a hippopotamus swimming next to her turns out to be a talking mouse. Alice has arrived in the absurdity of Wonderland, where she will encounter peculiar figures like the March Hare, the Cheshire Cat and the Mock Turtle. Speech and communication prove to be unreliable and reflect the dissolution of all rationality. Thus Alice gets the school verses she tries to recite all wrong and her dialogues with the Wonderland figures are condemned to failure. At any rate, Alice regains her ability to act during the tale when, with the help of the caterpillar, she learns how to control her size by eating pieces of mushroom and thus can explore all of the rooms.

The nameless protagonist of Will Self's story *Scale* (1995) also becomes smaller and smaller. In a drug-induced frenzy he falls into a crack in the road and down into a world where he loses all sense of proportion and scale. Not only does he shrink, but his surroundings shrink with him. In an opioid delirium, he finds himself amid children's dishes that his ex-wife left him after their separation and which he now begins using for morphine consumption. He muses on a remark his father once made about his books lacking any sense of scale, and reflects on the literary inspiration he gets from opiate before suddenly finding himself in a nightmarish situation. In his nocturnal frenzy, he enters ever deeper into a world of full of model constructions. "Some people lose their sense of proportion; I've lost my sense of scale"

(Self 1995: 3) explains the protagonist at the beginning, and as the story continues it becomes apparent that he has in fact not only lost all sense of scale but also of temperance and moderation and that in his drug-induced frenzy he is moving through a world that is getting smaller and smaller. Wasps look like zeppelins to him, and dust bunnies drift about like thundering avalanches. Analogous to the shrinking rooms, the protagonist continuously decreases in size, until he is as tiny as a subatomic particle and now fears he is becoming subject to Heisenberg's uncertainty principle, whereby he would stop existing as a whole entity. There is the danger that he will lose his self and thus the world.

Clash of dimensions

A clash of different systems of measurement is also presented in Jonathan Swift's satirical novel *Gulliver's Travels*

(1726). On his first journey, Gulliver is confronted with the Lilliputians, a tiny people in whose microcosm he has to find his way. The island inhabitants veer between admiration and fear of the "Man-Mountain" (Swift 1826: 40), as they call him, and the court has to employ a considerable number of staff to provide him with food (300 cooks!) and clothing (200 seamstresses). Accustomed power structures begin to crumble as Gulliver is now the biggest person in the empire. He himself idealises the miniature world, which he views from the bird's-eye perspective; the scenery of countryside and island residents seems perfect to him. The Lilliputians live in a world adapted to the dimensions of their bodies. The appropriateness of the proportions that functions within one's respective community fails in comparison to the size of the other. In his view, the Lilliputian world is microscopic, and what seems familiar becomes unidentifiable due to the reduction in size. Thus Gulliver cannot recognize with the naked eye the needle and thread of a sewing Lilliputian girl. At the same time, the size relations collapse when Gulliver, with the best intentions, puts out a fire that has broken out in the imperial palace with his huge stream of urine.

Gulliver experiences a complete shift of perspective on his next trip, to Brobdingnag, the land of the giants. Now he is suddenly the pipsqueak, who is scared stiff of the giants surrounding him. Seen from close up, proportions and symmetries change, the harmony is disrupted, beautiful and ugly become a question of perspective. All order of things is lost. The breasts of the wet nurse, which he would normally find attractive, now appear disgusting and monstrous to him. Unlike Alice, who constantly changes her size, or the shrinking protagonist in *Scale*, Gulliver constantly remains the same size.

But his surroundings change and thus so do the size relationships. With the scaling effects, the relativity of all knowledge and values becomes clear to Gulliver. Everything he sees and experiences stands in relation to his environment, whose benchmark is he himself. It is not the size differences per se that are problematic for Gulliver, but their interplay, which is marked by misunderstandings and prejudices.

While giants are usually depicted as being monstrous and horrifying, portrayals of little beings are usually positive, above all in legends and fairy tales. The small – imagined here in spatial terms – can contain very big things: the most beautiful treasures, clothing made of pure gold, and the most precious jewellery fall out of *Cinderella's* nut, and small people, animals or objects that have great strength unfold extraordinary powers. Thus the guardian of the hoard of the

Nibelungs is a *dwarf*, and the inconspicuous slippers of *Little Muck* function as seven-league boots and his little stick has great magical power because it can find buried treasure. It is not highly complex strategies that are needed to come up with solutions, but small, inconspicuous magic objects whose effect, however, is unfathomably great. Also among the well-known themes are unsolvable tasks that have to be carried out in a very short time. Thus King Augeas thinks it is not possible for *Heracles* to clean the stock-yard full of cow dung in just one day.

Under the magnifying glass

Hence a representation of scaling goes hand in hand with the understanding that all knowledge and positing of norms depends on the respective perspective. The question of the status of this perspective is often linked to the motif of perception, which is materialized in the object of an optical device. In literary texts, visual aids such as telescopes, microscopes, and magnifying glasses serve to make (hidden) contexts visible, and on the other hand to make the relativity of perception clear.[2] Peregrine Tyss, the protagonist of E.T.A. Hoffmann's literary fairy-tale *Master Flea* (1822), has to experience the visualization of an otherwise invisible world. With the microscope that is given to him by the leader of the fleas he can observe what other people are thinking, but he grapples with the realization that the states and thoughts of his interlocutors are not congruent, but often scheming and malicious.

Furthermore, the microscopic view serves to describe the grotesque and comical. In Friedrich Dürrenmatt's novella *Der Auftrag* (1986: 7, original in German) the husband transforms in the detailed

2 For the use of optical measuring devices, see Stadler (2003).

diary notes of his wife into a monster, “as if under a microscope, constantly narrowing and magnifying the focus”. The zoomed-in view is coupled with a loss of appreciation and marks a loss of reality that culminates in detailed, reciprocal observation by the couple. Irrespective of whether the scaling serves to illustrate or exaggerate, when the respective object is viewed more closely the conditions are invariably re-evaluated.

However, detailed insights are provided not only at the level of character descriptions, but also regarding the pace of the narration, the relationship between narrating time (i.e. the time needed to tell or read a narrative text), and narrated time (the period which is covered by a narration). Accelerated narration scales particularly by means of time jumps, gaps and condensing processes. Time-stretching narration, on the other hand, can be compared to looking through a magnifying glass. In Nicholson Baker's *The Mezzanine* (1988), an office clerk devotes himself to numerous details of everyday life. While riding on an escalator, Howie muses upon his torn shoelaces, drinking straws, men's magazines, a milk carton, his purchase of popcorn and much more. His obsession with detail is marked in the text by the interposition of exact descriptions and extensive reflections. At the same time, the protagonist continues to let his thoughts wander, which is reflected graphically in almost page-long footnotes. The footnotes also stand out visually because they are often longer than the main text. The narrative time in the novel advances continually, while the story itself comes to a standstill.

Of adequate size

Literary texts that present scaling negotiate values and examine knowledge and hierarchies; the result is often a loss of orientation. The scaling effects serve as catalysts in order to negotiate existential issues, as the examples provided have shown. And this can be quite funny at times. In Umberto Eco's satirical instruction manual *How to travel with a Salmon* (1986), it quickly becomes apparent that the monstrously large salmon will only cause problems in the hotel room. The protagonist receives an astronomically high bill at reception because the staff assumed that he had consumed huge quantities of spirits and snacks from the minibar. The hotel clerks are not interested in the fact that the first-person narrator removed several dozens of bottles, cans, and bags only temporarily to create space. Communication problems prevent the matter from being clarified. The publisher that has to foot the bill for the travel expenses is angry, the salmon can no longer be eaten, and the man's children suspect he has an alcohol problem.

The only thing that helps is humour. Or a magnum bottle of Scotch.

English translation by Burke Barrett

References

Baker, Nicholson, 1988, *The Mezzanine: A novel.* New York: Weidenfeld & Nicolson.

Brüder Grimm, 2009, *Kinder- und Hausmärchen*, Rölleke (ed.), Stuttgart: Reclam, publ. in English as *Grimm's fairy tales.* New York: Pantheon Books, 1945.

Carroll, Lewis, 2015, *Alice's Adventures in Wonderland.* Dover: Dover Thrift Edition (1865).

Dürrenmatt, Friedrich, 1986, *Der Auftrag.* Zurich: Diogenes, publ. in English as *The Assignment.* London: Cape, 1988.

Eco, Umberto, 1994, *How to Travel with a Salmon and Other Essays.* London: Secker, originally published in Italian as *Come viaggiare con un salmone* in 1986.

Genzmer, Felix, 1995, *Das Nibelungenlied*, Stuttgart: Reclam, publ. in English as *The Nibelungenlied.* Oxford: University Press, 2010.

Graves, Robert, 1992, *The Greek myths.* London: Penguin.

Hauff, Wilhelm, 2013, *Sämtliche Märchen*, ed. by Hans-Heino Ewers. Stuttgart: Reclam, publ. in English as *Hauff's Tales.* Sydney: William Brooks, 1949.

Hoffmann, E.T.A., 1826, *Specimens of German Romance; Vol. II. Master Flea.* London: Geo. B. Whittaker, originally published in German as *Meister Floh* in 1822.

Hustvedt, Siri, 2012, 'My Strange Head', in *Living, Thinking, Looking: Essays.* New York: Picador: 24–36.

Self, Will, 1995, *Scale.* London/New York: Penguin.

Stadler, Ulrich, 2003, *Der technisierte Blick: Optische Instrumente und der Status von Literatur; ein kulturhistorisches Museum.* Würzburg: Königshausen & Neumann.

Swift, Jonathan, 1826, *Gulliver's Travels.* London: Jones and Company (1726).

Mirjam Steiner (*1975, Zurich) is a literary and art scholar. She works as a research assistant at the Zurich University of the Arts.

Julie Harboe

On Human Scale and Calibrating Research Groups in a Wind Tunnel

Julie Harboe

On Human Scale and Calibrating Research Groups in a Wind Tunnel

During the last three years the art and research project 'Size Matters: On the Scale and Size of Models' has enabled a variety of experiments in and around the project's main instrument, a wind tunnel specifically constructed for the project. This wind tunnel, now on the roof of the Zurich University of the Arts (ZHdK), is not a perfect instrument. Rather, it is a model of a wind tunnel and somewhere between an artistic sketch and a scientific tool. It gives us a certain freedom to reflect on research as a common domain between the thought systems we apply for invention, innovation, serendipity, poetry, imagery, and so on.

The following text is an attempt at a metaphorical or speculative experiment developed to bring attention to how individual awareness of diverse forms of scale is essential for (future) dynamics of exchange. The experiment involves scaling and calibrating four research groups with the variables wind tunnels use to shape models. The resulting models of the groups' activities refer to – and may enhance – a discussion about research environments. The experiment also permits a U-turn making us aware that human in-scalability is an essential resource. Research (as well as art) is not about adjusting this resource to a system, but rather about allowing diverse insights and intuitions to merge or calibrate or collide for the sake of new insights.

A basic thesis explored here is that negotiation and interaction involve a form of scaling and constant adjustment. Artistic research, or research driven by open processes applying physical models and paying more attention to specific settings, may help us reverse or at least shake the supremacy of standardization and measurement by numbers, and offer us a new space and different methods to discuss values and quality. For this context, the ZHdK wind tunnel is an example of an acting and activating intermediary model. On the one hand it represents the scientific process, implies categories,and on the other, it is a work of art that reflects imperfection and uniqueness, frailty and inefficiency, which are associated with living creatures.

The key aspiration of the experiment is to make visible the interaction resulting from this dual character of the wind tunnel, and to claim that the focus on the potential and difficulties of constantly moving, exchanging and adjusting is necessary to bring us closer to a human scale as the basis for our co-existence, however impractical it may seem.

Research starts with human incentive and curiosity and in the last two centuries this has been efficiently brought to fruition and explored by bringing people together at universities and laboratories in increasingly controlled settings, where the research groups act as ultimate innovation instruments. Particularly in the last decades management of research and development environments, in both the public and the private sector, which is eager to accelerate, regulate and streamline innovation processes, seems to have lost touch with the human dimension upon which the research depends. Abstract evaluation systems have come to define quality and rewards. The focus is less on the researchers' interaction and the potential consequences of their research in a societal context and more on establishing efficient systems of production. New digital tools have added crowd-sourcing and citizen science to the ways in which we collaborate regarding scientific questions and added a public dimension to our understanding of the concept of collective innovation. However, it seems that the interests at stake and the algorithms used exclude rather than include essential dynamics of innovation (Wolf 2015). For better or for worse, human invention depends on collaboration and includes such unruly elements as empathy, chance, communication, respect and aesthetics. It is worthwhile searching for ways of seeing and negotiating these and many more essential components of the research environment. We need to re-adjust or change the conversation which has indiscernibly moved from constructing systems to adhering to them.

The experiment and the wind tunnel

Wind tunnels, like most scientific instruments, normally deal with a sense of scale that does not take into account human individuality and size. They are made to reproduce external phenomena of the movement of air around an object or an object's movement through the air at different regimes of scale and velocity. Hence, though the results of these experiments influence our environment, they do not relate to the fact that the main human force, as developed with the concept of *human rights*, is the irreducibility of our integrity and the right to limitless storms of imagination.

Wind tunnels deal with the likewise un-scalable and unruly wind[1] and their void is a strong metaphor for their role as a poetic and enigmatic catalyst that caters to inventiveness.[2] Can we use the wind tunnel to produce an experiment where, since the flow can be turned in the tunnel, we reverse the process by not testing an object or a model, but rather focusing on the conditions of testing itself? Can we use the view from the tunnel to re-boot our attention to the fundamental importance of human scale? Might this also empower us to think differently about scientific tools and the conditions for our different research domains?

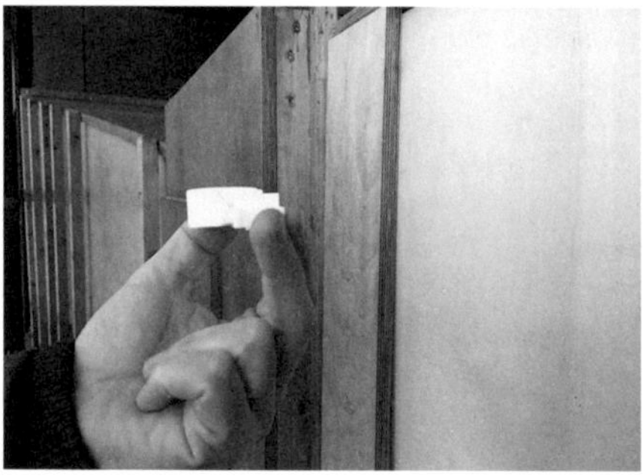

Fig. 1. ZHdK wind tunnel and its prototype (K. König).

The models

Wind tunnels may be tools of abstraction and reduction and they are important in today's science because they rely on materiality and the scientists' observations and offer dynamic and haptic elements of a different complexity than digital tools.

The wind tunnel works with shapes based on physical categories, as 'Size Matters' Artistic PhD candidate Haseeb Ahmed once explained while his professor of aeronautics, Olivier Chazot, was talking to the group on Skype from the Von Karman Institute in Brussels:

> Sometimes you have a scale model that looks very different from the 1:1 condition you are reproducing within the test section. This scaling is non-linear as there are the three variables and their balance has to be correct, but can be quite different:

1 For this parallel of the 'unscalable' wind I am indebted to Haseeb Ahmed, who as an open and critical reader has accompanied the writing of this text. I also wish to thank Ronny Hardliz for his useful comments.

2 This makes the wind tunnel a unique instrument and was the reason for Florian Dombois' choice of it for the 'Size Matters' project.

1) Form/scale of the model is determined in respect to the two variables below calculated in non-linear scaling equations[3].
2) Velocity
3) Viscosity of the fluid, i.e. air, is fixed but has different effects on the objects depending on scales or temperatures. (Personal notes from 2 February 2015)

The experiment attempted in this paper is to apply the wind tunnel's variables of *size, time* and *energy* as the basis for researching the environments of four research groups active during the last 15 years. The models were developed to turn attention from the products of the groups' research to the interaction and conditions of the researchers themselves.[4]

The groups modelled are all inter- or transdisciplinary constellations positioned between art and scientific research and educational environments working at the fringes of mainstream research. What they all have in common is a distinct institutional and individual autonomy. In the eye of the academic tempest, they were or are driven by artists and researchers with particularly strong intrinsic motivation and their diversity seems to make them particularly resistant to *standardization*.

Collapsing work environments of research groups into models based on the above criteria is, as mentioned, a way to redirect and reverse our attention. The models work with and reflect our individual gaze[5] and the viewers' subjective reactions act as a substitute for the loss of specificity. Art research or artistic research offers an appropriate loophole to do this as it is open to singular interpretation (Badura, Dubach et al. 2015).

The research groups

The models here representing (a) Collegium Helveticum, Zurich 1997–2004, (b) Art Research Unit in Lucerne 2007–2012, (c) Future Laboratory CreaLab 2011–Present, and (d) 'Size Matters' Research Project Zurich 2013–2015 are supplemented by short descriptions to enable the models to impact you as a viewer. Form and size refer to the physical spaces or models of spaces the groups were working in. Time refers to the general time frame of collaborations; and energy depicts the format or specific quality of the groups' interaction.

3 The Navier-Stokes equation enables the integration and calculation of the dynamic regime (cf. Olivier Chazot's essay in this volume: 193–208).

4 A detailed description of the four groups and their work can be found in a first approach to this scaling experiment in a paper for the Transvaluation Symposium in Göteborg, May 2015 (http://conferences.chalmers.se/index.php/Transvaluation/Transvaluation/paper/viewFile/1864/554, accessed 15 March 2016).

5 The models were made by the author, who was part of all research groups. Using the variables from the wind tunnel is a way of camouflaging the fact that making such models inevitably implies a portion of subjective interpretation. However, the concepts are not haphazard; they help providing insight into the basic conditions for research projects.

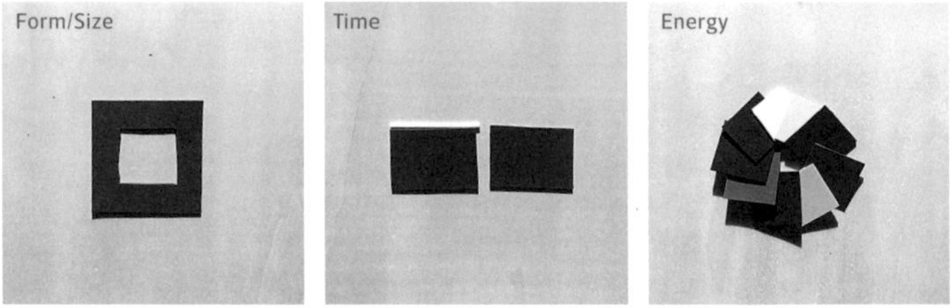

Collegium Helveticum, Zurich 1997–2004

This research group was an institute and used to be located with the Chair of Philosophy of Science at the Zurich-based Swiss Federal Institute of Technology (ETHZ). Each year a new diverse group made up of PhD students or postdocs came together to exchange ideas and work on a general theme that reflected on science in society and transdisciplinary methodologies. In the model you see *Form/Size* as a brown open square, merging as a symbol the wooden spaces of the ETHZ Sternwarte in Zurich and the classical academic seminar arrangement with tables organised in a square. *Time* was split into two semesters. The first included a visual artist, whose work opened the forum to discussing art contexts, symbolized here by a light blue line. The *energy* of the Collegium is shown as an intense circular format dominated by written academic input.

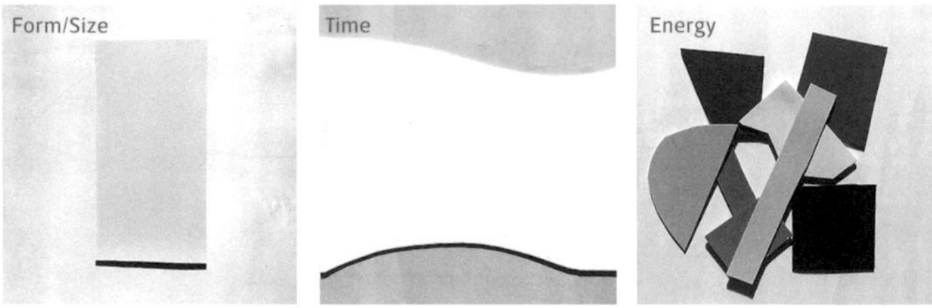

Art Research Unit 2007–2012

Artists, professors, lecturers, assistants and PhD students of the Faculty of Fine Arts made up a new research unit at Lucerne University of Sciences and Arts (LUASA) (Harboe 2010). The group had neutral (grey) office spaces at their disposal with no possibility to do messy studio-like work. This limited the encounters to organizational exchange, reading or discussion, far removed from practice. The timeframe of the collaborations can be seen as a river where the artists dive into, share, and work on projects but with no specific common frame. This is positive combined with the energy that emerges from the meeting of diverse individual oeuvres as individual shapes in motion.

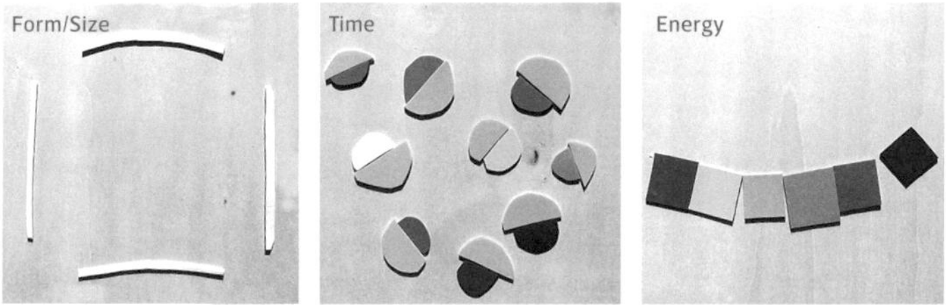

Future Laboratory CreaLab 2011–Present

The CreaLab started as an interdisciplinary research initiative of LUASA. Professors and lecturers from all departments come together to conduct and support practice-based research on how to manage innovation processes (Meissner et al. 2015). The group has no fixed place to meet or work. A fine outline represents the border of the group's space of interaction. The juggling two-coloured balls describe how CreaLab works from project to project, teaming up with different partners. *Action Research* is the keyword for the work and the continued transfer of energy between the collaborators is essential. The work is based on trust and reciprocity and the certainty that members will *receive a kick* or impulse from the different members driving and sharing the energy of the group.

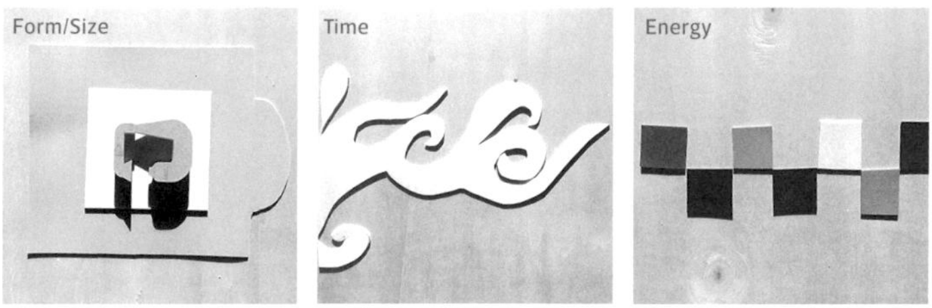

'Size Matters' Research Project 2013–2015

The wind tunnel research group, hosting the *Too Big to Scale* symposium, is composed of seven or eight people (not all are directly funded by the project). The project is part of the transdisciplinary research focus at the ZHdK. It is the smallest group of the four groups analysed here. The *Form/Size* space is defined by the wind tunnel, though it should be noted that its position on the roof of ZHdK's new Toni Areal building, seen here as a grey shape or shadow, has had a dominant effect on the project. *Time* here evolves in a stylized and ornamental way, a bit like a vortex (cf. Haseeb Ahmed in this volume: 177–192), to express the unity and that the inner core of the project is visual and not based on abstract or theoretical hypotheses. The *energy* of the group is defined by the abstract staircase of the *Fahrkunst* (Wind Tunnel Bulletin #4, 2015) where the different competences of the group members jump between practical or performative and theoretical tasks in workshops, experiments with and around the wind tunnel, and publications.

On the other side of the *palaver* paravent

At the symposium *Too Big to Scale*, the presentation of this paper consisted of an introduction with photos of the visualisations beamed on the paravent. The audience then moved to the other side of the paravent to encounter the models on their 30 cm x 30 cm plates (fig. 2–5) with the loosely coloured shapes laid out on the floor. The physical presence of the models clearly facilitated the discussion about the impressions, and the reactions indicated that the audience present imagined how working in and under the different conditions would impact them. The images also inspired desires, for instance, to be part of the bouncing encounters of the CreaLab *Time* model, or to be in the completely neutral space of the Art Research Unit's *Form/Size* model. Moreover, this was also the place to reflect the size of the groups as the number of members would be the most obvious understanding of the *scale* of a research group. The three first groups (a), (b), and (c) are more or less the same size, 18–20 individuals, indicating the commonly acknowledged size of groups engaged in active exchange. However, when we look at the models it becomes clear that the *Form/Size* reference reflected the institutional context, the spaces, more than the number of people engaged. Hence the dense academic context of the Collegium Helveticum model, the stretched and neutral space of the Art Research Unit, the almost invisible space of the CreaLab *Form/Size* model, as well as the layered form of the smaller 'Size Matters' group (d) on top of the silhouette of the Toni Areal building, all show that the research groups operate on different physical *scales* depending on the dispositions of their spaces. Such insights enable us to approach diverse dimensions essential to the conditions of research environments, and offer a basis for candid evaluation formats.

Four narratives as models

The four scaling experiments above represent an overview of some institutional and individual circumstances of research groups. They could be reproduced for other groups or contexts. Moreover, they represent a way of understanding the workings of models not in their capacity to reproduce or reduce a given object, nor pointing to a possible future reality, but rather as active objects interacting and facilitating a negotiation and depending on subjective interaction (Mahr 2008). As such, they leave it up to us to develop modes of cooperation according to our human scale.

The following four *narratives* represent additional perspectives on the circumstances of research groups. As opposed to the models, the narratives convey four instances of concrete information and observation bringing us closer to the discussions around the issue of the conditions of research groups.

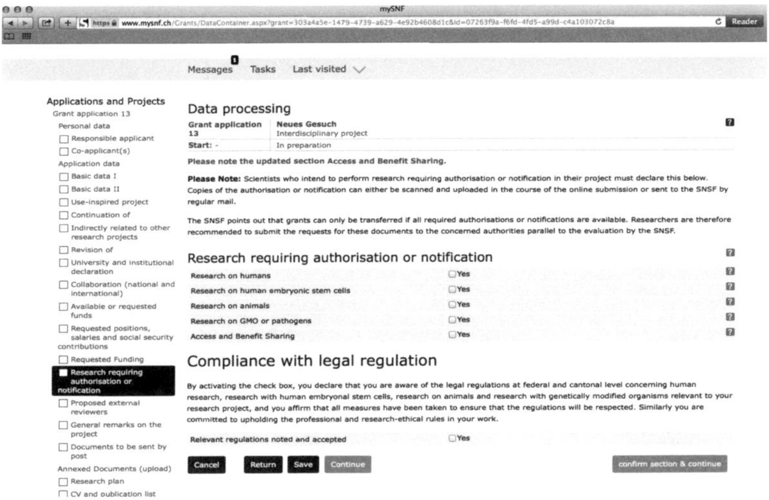

Fig. 6. Screenshot of the SNSF online application tool.

Reversing streamlined research

One afternoon a few years ago in the grey offices of an art school's research department, a question popped up on the screen of the online application tool of the Swiss National Science Foundation (SNSF) *mysnf*: were we doing *research on humans*? The team around the computer in that intense moment almost ticked the box. The question made us aware of the fact that the process of adjusting the project to the framework of the SNSF could be seen as a bureaucratic experiment with our thoughts, our intellectual freedom and our motivation.

In several contributions, the economist Mathias Binswanger has shown that the culture of application writing is neither meaningful nor motivating or sustainable from a financial or human-resources point of view (Binswanger 2012). Did this flipping of the perspective we had experienced in front of the screen show us how such framing adjusts, exploits and scales the researcher rather than supporting innovation? It is tempting to compare the streamlining of objects in the wind tunnel to how applications are adjusted by the flows of the research agencies rather than formed by the intention and objectives of the researchers. In this context it is, however, positive that there are examples of changes in application culture. The European Research Council invites contesters whose proposals have passed step 1 to meet the selection committee in person. Moreover, in Finland it has been shown that complex interdisciplinary projects fare better when proposals are discussed openly and the evaluators are included in the decision-making process (Raaska 2011).

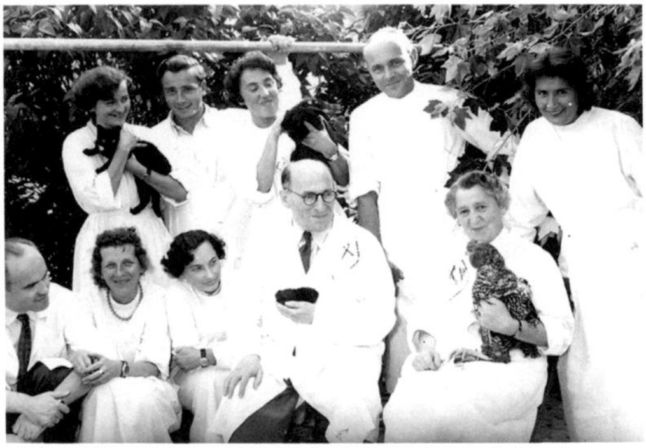

Fig. 7 Fleck and research group before 1957 (AfZ:FD Thomas Schnelle/9).

Fleck's listening

The issue of how we do research and interact in order to find new forms of knowledge was a central point in Ludwik Fleck's contribution and his extensive writings on the philosophy of science from an empirically- and practice-based point of view. He tried to turn attention from the passive system of knowledge work dominated by methods/conventions to the dynamics of the engaged scientist or researcher using his or her skills and intuitions in collaborative negotiation with colleagues as thought collectives.

In *Entstehung und Entwicklung einer wissenschaftlichen Tatsache (Genesis and Development of a Scientific Fact)* Fleck describes the finding of the Wassermann reaction, which changed the study of bacteria. In the text we are introduced to the scientists' environments and methods and come to understand how difficult it is to break habits of thinking and seeing. Fleck describes how the underlying processes that help us understand the material cannot immediately be formulated by the researcher and, as the first step of cognition does not present any conclusions, the process must be understood as something close to listening to 'an inner tune', an understanding that makes the conditions of the researcher comparable to those of an artist, as it were (Fleck 1935/1980: 113). This first sense of cognition can only be defined in hindsight through the results. The initial perception takes place in an intuitive space and offers no linear development. This melody, as Fleck defines it, which the individual researcher listens to and gradually tunes in to, is fundamentally different from a scientific tool. In his texts Fleck clearly describes this process of observation and how it is connected with both the interaction of the scientists and the importance of observing a material reality.

One could say that Fleck focuses attention on the human ability to look for different scales and elaborates on this by describing the fluidity of scientific method. Fleck's approach shows that operating on this human scale is complicated and depends on people's ability to interact in a group and not be too satisfied with the status quo, however successful the known solution or powerful the backing of a particular paradigm in the community is (Fleck 1935/1980: 122).

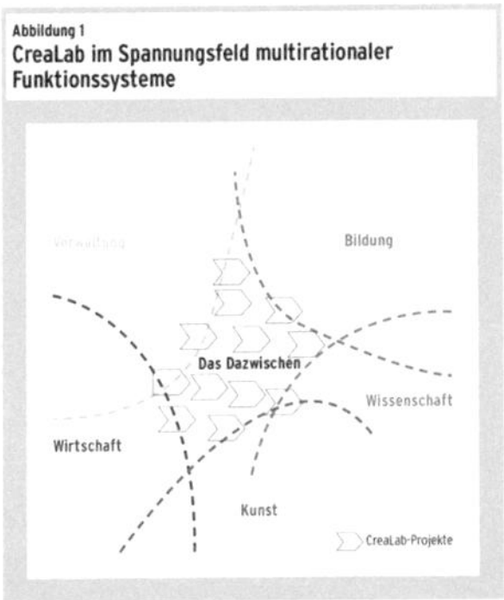

Fig. 8 Illustration from Meissner et al. 2015.

Collaboration – in between

Jens Meissner, Patricia Wolf and the author of this essay wrote an article about CreaLab, the action research group the three of us have been part of since 2011 (Meissner et al. 2015). CreaLab, described above, started as an interdisciplinary research focus at Lucerne University of Applied Sciences and Arts (LUASA) and came to represent an institutional non-space or *in-between*. LUASA is one of the most thoroughly organized educational institutions in Switzerland, as is confirmed by its EFQM certificates. However, the CreaLab brought together a group of people who worked based on their competences, curiosity and an inner need to exchange ideas across the university's formal discipline-based organisation. The article describes how the core team navigated the institution's "multi-rational" interests. It makes clear that the institution's space, time and energy are calibrated by the authority of the institution using finances as its decisive scaling instrument. The analysis of CreaLab's development can be read as an expression of a crisis of scale (cf. Reinhard Wendler in this volume: 65–80) between the human values of energy and interaction in the group and the economic framework. When the group is forced to find new ways of defining their work they develop new spaces in between different rationalities and stay flexible and innovative. Though motivation and innovation can also be modelled, the premises of this independent and actively exchanging group function differently – more like wind than like objects within the institution.

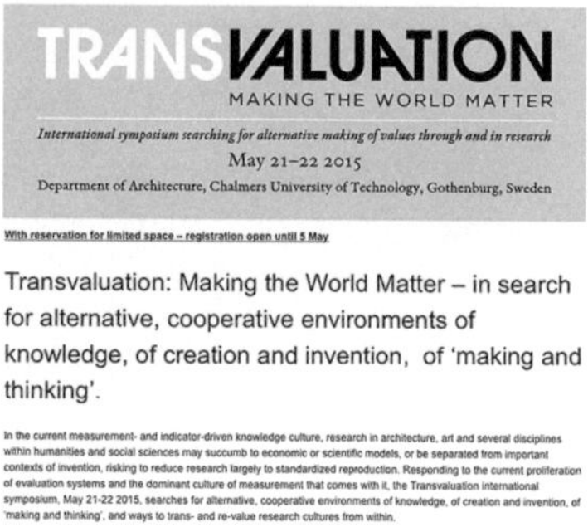

TRANSVALUATION
MAKING THE WORLD MATTER

International symposium searching for alternative making of values through and in research

May 21–22 2015

Department of Architecture, Chalmers University of Technology, Gothenburg, Sweden

With reservation for limited space – registration open until 5 May

Transvaluation: Making the World Matter – in search for alternative, cooperative environments of knowledge, of creation and invention, of 'making and thinking'.

In the current measurement- and indicator-driven knowledge culture, research in architecture, art and several disciplines within humanities and social sciences may succumb to economic or scientific models, or be separated from important contexts of invention, risking to reduce research largely to standardized reproduction. Responding to the current proliferation of evaluation systems and the dominant culture of measurement that comes with it, the Transvaluation international symposium, May 21-22 2015, searches for alternative, cooperative environments of knowledge, of creation and invention, of 'making and thinking', and ways to trans- and re-value research cultures from within.

Fig. 9 Transvaluation.

Transvaluation

Finally, a call for proposals for a symposium on transvaluation in May 2015 at Chalmers University in Gothenburg addressed the changing relationship between individuals and institutions asking participants directly to focus *on making the world matter, on cooperative environments of knowledge, on creation, invention, and on 'making and thinking'.*

The team behind the symposium expanded on this in a statement that tied into to a critique of research culture similar to the examples above.

> In the current measurement and indicator-driven knowledge culture, research in architecture, art, and several disciplines within the humanities and social sciences may succumb to economic or scientific models, or be separated from important contexts of invention, risking to reduce research largely to standardized reproduction. Responding to the current proliferation of evaluation systems and the dominant culture of measurement that comes with it, the Transvaluation symposium [...] searches for alternative, cooperative environments of knowledge, of creation and invention, of 'making and thinking', and ways to trans- and re-value research cultures from within.[6]

The call prompted the experiment described in this essay with the models of the groups as a different kind of evaluation tool. The models should help us see the role of collaboration formats as meaningful points of departure. Using the criteria of size, time and energy reverses the obsession in applications culture with standardization and evaluation of goals and results. The

6 Online at http://www.chalmers.se/en/departments/arch/research/Conferences/Transvaluation%20Symposium/Pages/default.aspx (accessed 30 January 2017).

models show us how changing from a focus on a fictive future to an appreciation of context, options and energy with relation to both the individuals involved and the subject matter – addressed here as human scale – might present a much more relevant basis for evaluating a project's future worth.

The above shorthand narratives show us in a compact way that it is relevant to 1) resist the streamlining of research and the wasting of resources as Binswanger points out, 2) pay attention to the *inside* of the research process as Fleck did, and 3) move actively in between the institutional logics as in the case of the Future Laboratory CreaLab. Furthermore 4) the Transvaluation initiative's insistence on showing, making and thinking reflects the general argument of this essay. All are strong arguments for altering the way research is organized.

Situating human scale

For the *Too Big to Scale* symposium, the aerodynamic terminology was tweaked into a call for contributions relating to the more humanistic terms of *size, time, energy* (cf. introduction to this volume). The title of the conference calls to mind Sigfried Giedion's *Space, Time and Architecture* (Giedion 1941). The book stands as a monument to a new understanding of architectural history developed in the early 20th century. Particularly when seen in the context of aerodynamics and wind studies, we understand how Giedion's approach to architecture, rather than being a *detached* investigation of style or symbolic form or a history of technical developments, enables us to follow the wind around the corners and register anew how we move between buildings, relocating the experience to our bodies. This physical dimension seems central to the discussion about how to (re-)locate or intertwine our imagination in the research system with respect to the human dimension.

Today we are acquainted with and aware of diverse processes of scaling. In any interaction – be it judging quality or the proportions of things – we zoom in and out, reflecting on how much is appropriate in a given context, registering our own size between the bus shed and the skyscraper, or the opportunities the number on our bank account provides. However, some forms of scaling are more difficult to grasp than others. Crudely formulated, scientific tests may establish the *breaking point* of a specific material to be used for in stance in buildings or bridges (cf. Reinhard Wendler in this volume: 65–80), or we can grasp the consequences of the scaling of relations we define as systems (cf. Frank Schweitzer in this volume: 161–176). The social sciences have established access to ways of *bundling* subjective chaos into comprehensive data by means of qualitative research methods (Denzin and Lincoln 2005), and the movement around science and technology studies with Bruno Latour, Lorraine Daston, Steven Shapin and Isabel Stengers – to mention key protagonists in the field – contributed to an understanding that relates the laboratory to the philosophical implications of science and knowledge production.

However, attention to human scale requires methods that go beyond those developed over the last hundred and fifty years. If we want to foster an active discussion concerning the quality of interaction, we need to transcend the traditional word-by-word, number-by-number, line-by-line environment.

We can see from other contributions in this book that there is a strong tension in the discussion between the concept of scale as a physical phenomenon and the impact scaling has on our understanding of decisions and dynamics of other contexts. In other words, references to changes of scale seize our imagination, something which authors of fiction have played with actively for ages (cf. Mirjam Steiner in this volume: 97–112). The wind tunnel as an instrument contains a history of this and offers us an opportunity to reflect the transformation that takes place in the shaping and scaling of objects. In its normal experiments the "Wind Tunnel World" (cf. Haseeb Ahmed in this volume: 177–192) enables us to see a future and render the consequences of our thoughts and actions more palpable. The wind tunnel has accompanied the dream of flying, the fulfilment of this dream, and the expansion of air traffic up to the current scale where the eruption of the volcano Eyafjallajökull grounded thousands of planes and left tons of freshly cut flowers for the US market to rot in Kenyan greenhouses.

Conclusion

Scaling is about assessing an adequate (or inadequate) relation between physical or psychological components. The wind tunnel's intriguing implications, drawn from its capacity to create, shape and seduce researchers into materializing more or less deadly inventions, show how important it is to have mental scope and to put up resistance, and they demonstrate how efficient a practice of form-finding can be with prototypes of all kinds, even research groups.

The visualisation of the four research groups modelled here offers us a different view of the framing of research and some of the properties of the groups in comparison. The models enable a change of perspective so that we might both imagine what it means to work in research groups and focus on a discussion about the dynamics and centrality of collaborative formats: What is the role of the form and space in which the research takes place? How does the timeframe impact on the work? And which formats of interaction generate a specific energy and environment that is positive for innovation? The above models are particularly useful because they were all examples of groups where radical innovation and academic freedom and openness played or play an important role in their formation of knowledge.

This reframing of the evaluation of research proposals from a process focused on scientific tools and results, to a focus on *human scale*, making visible the individual contributions and conditions of our work, brings us back to a discourse about research that is accessible, not played out in an abstract line-by-line argument or shaped by financial or institutional trajectories and losing track of the actual interaction and the consequences of the research. The models presented here are humble close-ups of aspects of refined collaborations. The models reverse the wind tunnel's efficiency: they do not represent a streamlined product, reducing risk and resistance, but rather expand uncertainty and stress the turmoil of the encounter which is research. Instead of using the wind tunnel to calibrate our surroundings, this reverse approach challenges us to address and deal with the incommensurable human scale, including the grandeur of nature, and demand that we negotiate a space to do essential, airy, blue-sky research work.

References

Binswanger, Matthias, 2012, *Sinnlose Wettbewerbe: Warum wir immer mehr Unsinn produzieren.* Freiburg/Basel/Wien: Herder.

Badura, Jens, Selma Dubach et al. (eds.), 2015, *Künstlerische Forschung: Ein Handbuch.* Berlin: Diaphanes.

Denzin, Norman K., and Yvonna S. Lincoln, 2011, *The SAGE Handbook of Qualitative Research.* London: Sage.

Fleck, Ludwik, 1980, *Entstehung und Entwicklung einer wissenschaftlichen Tatsache.* Frankfurt a. M.: Suhrkamp Verlag (1935).

Giedion, Sigfried, 1941, *Space, Time and Architecture: The Growth of a New Tradition.* Cambridge: Harvard University Press.

Harboe, Julie, 2010, 'Art-Driven Research: Art Projects in New Frameworks' in *Art and Artistic Research,* Corina Caduff et al. (eds.). Zurich: Scheidegger & Spiess: 190–199.

Harboe, Julie, 'Werk und Prozess' in Badura, Jens, Selma Dubach et al. (eds.), *Künstlerische Forschung: Ein Handbuch.* Berlin: Diaphanes: 243–247.

Mahr, Bernd, 2008, 'Ein Modell des Modellseins: Ein Beitrag zur Aufklärung des Modellbegriffs' in Dirks, Ulrich, and Eberhard Knobloch (eds.), *Modelle.* Berlin: Lang.

Meissner, Jens, Patricia Wolf and Julie Harboe, 2015, 'Im "Dazwischen": Die Reise des Aktionsforschungsprogramms "CreaLab" durch die Multirationalität der Hochschulwelt' in *OrganisationsEntwicklung: Zeitschrift für Unternehmensentwicklung und Change Management* 2: 23–30.

Raaska, Laura, 2011, *Inter- and Multidisciplinary Project Proposals in the Fields of Biosciences and the Environment.* Online at http://www.transdisciplinarity.ch/td-net/Konferenzen/Vergangene-Konferenzen/2011/ITD 2011/mainColumnParagraphs/0/text_files/file/document/Booklet_2011_webFINAL.pdf (accessed 20 March 2016).

Wind Tunnel Bulletin #4. Fahrkunst. 2015, Zurich. Online at http://windtunnelbulletin.zhdk.ch/issue-04/ (accessed 30 January 2017).

Wolf, Patricia, 2015, 'Lokal, global, glokal: neue kollaborative Arbeitsformen' in *Computerworld* (7 May 2015): 36–37.

Julie Harboe is an art historian, critic and curator. Among other tasks she co-founded and managed an art space, developed and coordinated a unit for artistic research and is currently a lecturer at Future Laboratory CreaLab and Lucerne School of Business. She focuses on transdisciplinary collaborations in research, education, business and art.

Simon Grand and Christoph Weckerle

A Palaver on Scaling Creative Enterprises

Simon Grand and Christoph Weckerle
A Palaver on Scaling Creative Enterprises

Conceptual Perspective: "Controversial Issues" (Proposal)

(1) Discursive Context

In current debates on the future of the creative economies, we can observe the recurrent claim that the successful transformation of precarious activities, individual-centred businesses and local scenes into cultural, economic, political or societal value creation requires more detailed reflection, exploration and elaboration (Spinosa, Flores and Dreyfus 2001; Düllo and Liebl 2005; Martel 2010). In parallel, management approaches addressing this issue are often seen as problematic, given the processual, idiosyncratic, context-specific and often non- or anti-economic qualities of many enterprises and initiatives in the creative economies (Boltanski and Chiapello 1999; Reckwitz 2012). As a consequence, research, practice and policy must learn to better understand organizational processes and practices in artistic value creation, which are often characterized by experimentation with alternative economies and related strategies (Toma and Barrientos 2008).

Research that advances our understanding of such economies develops in different directions: (1) it explores the relationship between informal and formal modes of organizing; (2) it discusses the interplay and contradiction between singularity (Karpik 2010) and mainstream (Martel 2010); (3) it studies the formation of distributed communities and collective movements (Hess and Ostrom 2007); (4) it analyses creative organizing and alternative institutionalizations (Spinosa, Flores and Dreyfus 2001); (5) it studies critical companies as a way of reconsidering the concept of enterprise for art and culture (Toma and Barrientos 2008). These approaches have in common an interest in developing alternative modes of organizing and strategizing, which we develop further in our performative exploration by critically revisiting and reframing current, predominant views, as well as speculating about novel perspectives and practices.

(2) Research Focus

We discuss these processes through the perspective of *scaling*. Analogies typical for discussions on scaling in management with reference to physical artefacts and hardware more generally are of limited relevance here (Sutton and Rao 2014). Instead, we discuss scaling from the perspective of analogies from the digital realm, characterized by scaling strategies including reuse (Shifman 2014), copying (von Gehlen 2011), hacking (Düllo and Liebl 2005), open source (Lessing 1999), and automation (Maeda 2004). It is evident that these perspectives on scaling share an interest in the processuality of scaling as it unfolds over time (Langley 1999). In our performative exploration, we speculate how such patterns could be translated into a description or reframing of entrepreneurial organizational processes in the creative economies (Spinosa, Flores and Dreyfus 2001).

This has implications for research, as we have learnt from various contributions to the symposium. Scaling processes often cannot be approached as well-defined, generalizable sequences of actions, steps or phases in a linearized causal contingency model, but must be understood as a dynamic mapping of highly situated and context-specific, idiosyncratic potentialities (Langley 1999), which might emerge into and shape larger-scale outcomes in terms of spatial, temporal or societal impact (see also the other contributions and concluding discussions to the symposium). By identifying, discussing and mapping potentially relevant patterns, our contribution explores the possibilities for developing alternative research approaches to scaling (Grand and Jonas 2012). In doing so, we suggest complementing the careful description of scaling processes as they are by experimenting with alternative scaling possibilities as they could be.

This is also what we explore in our research collaboration with heterogeneous groups of actors in the creative economies, including researchers, policy makers, executives, and entrepreneurs (for further information, see www.creativeeconomies.com). In our performative exploration, we retell some stories of this collaboration, in particular about working with different moments of zooming in and zooming out that have allowed us to reframe current perspectives on the creative economies and enterprises as well as experiment with our own views.

Performative Exploration:
"From the Other Side of the Wall" (Presentation)

(0) Setting for the presentation

We present our performative exploration in the exhibition zone of the two separated spaces of the 'palaver' constellation developed by the symposium organizers. In this presentational format, the audience follows the presentation while sitting in the discussion zone, which is separated from the exhibition zone by a wall, or paravent. What the audience sees is a series of graphics on a TV screen; what they hear are our voices.

(1) Opening

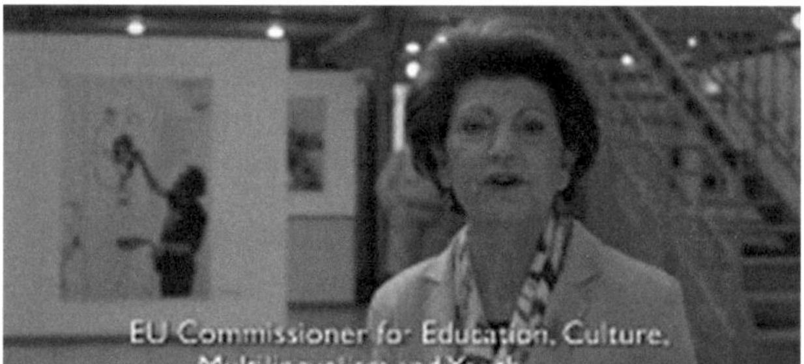

Video still 1 (the former EU Commissioner Androulla Vassiliou in a video promoting the Creative Europe Programme 2014–2020: © European Commission)

(2) First Part: Macro Perspectives on the Creative Industries
"This is how the European Commission describes the Cultural and Creative Industries (CCI): as an ordinary industrial sector with first and foremost a huge potential for growth and scaling. The standard vocabulary of economic development agencies is used. The discussion is about an increasing number of jobs, about turnover getting more and more important; it is a discussion about how a small company can become a big company.

The time that the European Commission launched this video in 2011 was also the moment when Simon and I decided to join forces and start a research initiative on the CCI, because the reality of the students from the Zurich University of the Arts (ZHdK), their work and thought processes and practices, and their visions all had very little to do with the content of this video. Our research links micro and macro perspectives. We observe countries and institutions on the one hand and creative actors and their practices and processes on the other.

In a way, we are constantly scaling up and down. Referring to the introduction given by Florian [Dombois] yesterday, the models you will see subsequently were models *on* the CCI in the beginning and then became models *for* the CCI, since we have been testing them not only in Europe but also in other parts of the world, mainly in Hong Kong – a global city where we could expose our ideas to a completely different context, which forced us to reframe many of our ideas. Thus our understanding regarding value creation, for example, has undergone serious modifications and the boundaries between well-established areas in the cultural sector, such as public or private, have been blurred through many interviews we conducted.

What are the impacts of the European Commission's arguments? On the one hand, the scaling option makes the CCI very attractive to politicians and decision makers and their agenda; on the other hand, many artists and designers don't

see themselves as part of the CCI because they have a different understanding of scaling that does not fit in with large parts of the economy. This is true, for example, for the size of an enterprise in the CCI, where growth is not always a desirable aim, or for working modes, which very often involve temporary constellations rather than stable structures suitable for long-term development.
Let us take a closer look: the concept of the CCI is modelled and visualized differently for different regions of the world: many circles for federalist countries, one circle with a clear midpoint for centralistic countries, triangles with the CCI at the top for regions where heavy industries are still the foundation of welfare, arrows for regions where CCI are understood as a powerful value chain, overlapping circles for the position between the corporate sector and the cultural sector (see fig. 1).

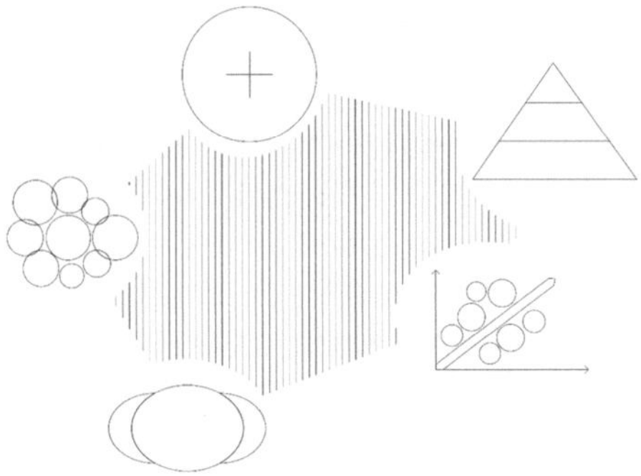

Fig. 1

The main purpose of these models is to reduce complexity. Zooming out means zooming away from the reality of the CCI. The result is a gap between the processes and practices of creative actors and the understanding of politicians. The CCI are far from being a constellation with well-defined sequences of actions in a linear model, since they are defined by a set of submarkets that sometimes have very little in common. This constitutes a dramatic challenge for traditional (mechanical) politics, governance and management. The CCI are more like a complex landscape that requires accurate mapping.

This means tolerating complexity and zooming in. What we observe through zooming in are force fields. One of the main drivers of CCI is the force field "singularity vs. mainstream". Every artist, every designer wants to be unique and distinctive; they want to do something no one else has done before. On the other hand, they want to have access to the market and this is where the mainstream element comes in. The audience has to get information about the singularity, wants to buy more than one of a kind, wants to compare it to other products or pieces of art, wants to know how much it costs, and so on.

Other characteristic force fields are: formal – informal, public – private, for profit – not for profit, tradition – innovation. What these force fields have in common is that they don't follow an either/or logic but more of a both/and logic. It's not singularity or mainstream. It's always both.

Taking the notion of these force fields seriously means not only expanding – as the European Commission does – but also focusing. For us this means not only zooming out, but also zooming in. This entails a shift away from the questions "What belongs to the CCI? How to measure the impact of the CCI?" towards "Who are the CCI? What are creative actors doing and why?"

And this is the perfect moment to switch voices and give the floor to Simon, who has been doing research by zooming in on selected creative enterprises by using micro approaches.

(3) Second Part: Micro Insights into Artistic Processes and Practices

Thank you, Christoph. First of all, it is important to note that while politicians and statisticians are discussing the CCI as an important phenomenon, the creative, entrepreneurial actors in the field itself do not see themselves as actors belonging to the CCI: they run design agencies, realize films, engage in artistic performances, develop computer games, and so on. Hence zooming in implies that the broad political, economical and cultural debates about the CCI move into the background, and what we see instead is the multitude and heterogeneity of highly idiosyncratic and specific practices, initiatives and related modes of organizing and managing artistic processes and their outcomes.

We observe a recurrent insistence on the singularity of these practices, initiatives and approaches, which on the one hand requires a detailed, in-depth research approach in order to cover the specificities and context-dependent features of such practices. On the other hand, it is nevertheless interesting, albeit provocative, to generalize and argue that although the approaches observed are very heterogeneous, some patterns can still be discerned.

Specifically, we can identify the following practices and strategies, which seem to characterize many artistic processes and organizations (see fig. 2):

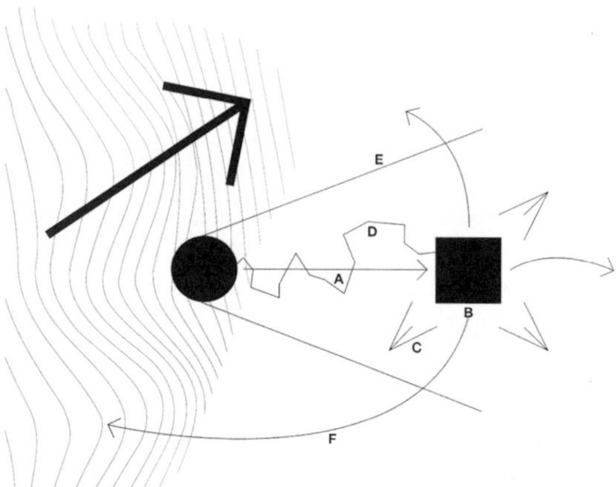

Fig. 2

A: They are about *pro-jecting*, meaning that they do not focus primarily on the world as it is, but rather on the world as it could be: alternative futures, alternative possibilities, alternative modes of organizing, and alternative institutions. At the same time, focusing on alternatives intrinsically implies criticizing, questioning and challenging the world as it is: this explains the inherently critical, subversive and speculative qualities of artistic processes.
B: Since such pro-jections are often fragile and can be very controversial, it is important to materialize them in the form of sketches, models, images, prototypes, and so on, in order to render them tangible, imaginable and thus accessible to further exploration and experimentation. This explains why the material, bodily, media-related aspect is so central to artistic processes: it is through, in and by actually *performing* alternative futures that they are explored and made accessible for negotiation.
C: Thus every artistic pro-jection is contingent: it could be otherwise, and it has to claim and confirm its ambition and quality as an artistic contribution. As a consequence, judgement processes are essential, mobilizing different *valuation devices*, including personal opinions, formal rankings, price mechanisms, curatorial interpretations and many more. The contingency of artistic projections explains the central role and the controversial nature of any such valuation device.
D: In order to advance and further develop artistic projections, multiple ways and *modes of experimentation*, bricolage, improvisation, and so on can be observed, which contribute to testing and advancing initial propositions and ideas. While materializations are understood as hypotheses or propositions, experiments and improvisations more or less systematically explore the potential relevance of these propositions and ideas, at the same time withdrawing, replacing or further sharpening them. In doing so, artistic actors and collectives develop their own and specific repertoire of experimentation arrangements.

E: Over time, such experimentation repertoires and related repertoires of creative practices, artistic tools and speculative strategies emerge into specific *organizational arrangements*, taking the form of artistic collectives, design agencies, creative networks, and subversive movements. In all these different cases, the common pattern is the transition from individual projects to a series of projections, initiatives and outcomes, a series which becomes an artistic position.
F: Accordingly, such an organizational arrangement, as well as the related positioning, has to be seen in a *multitude of economic, cultural and societal contexts*, which are explicitly or implicitly referred to in artistic practice. From the multitude of interactions, connections, translations and references emerging over time, an artistic position, its organizational institutionalization, its valuation and impact evolve. The above implies that artistic practices do not primarily confirm and stabilize the creative field described and identified as CCI from a macro perspective, but rather alter, challenge, change and reinvent this creative field with every new project, initiative and shift. It is thus interesting to explore whether and how this dynamic can become relevant for the further exploration of the CCI from a macro perspective as well.
And this is the perfect moment to switch speakers and hand the microphone over to Christoph, who has been debating these implications with many different institutions, as well as the question of whether and how these insights can become relevant outside the CCI in a narrow sense.

(4) Third Part: From CCI to the Creative Economies and their Spheres

Thank you, Simon. Since we have gone into some detail, let's now zoom out again and ask ourselves whether and how all this relates to other areas of knowledge and production. Are there creative enterprises outside the CCI in the strict sense defined by the British Department for Culture, Media

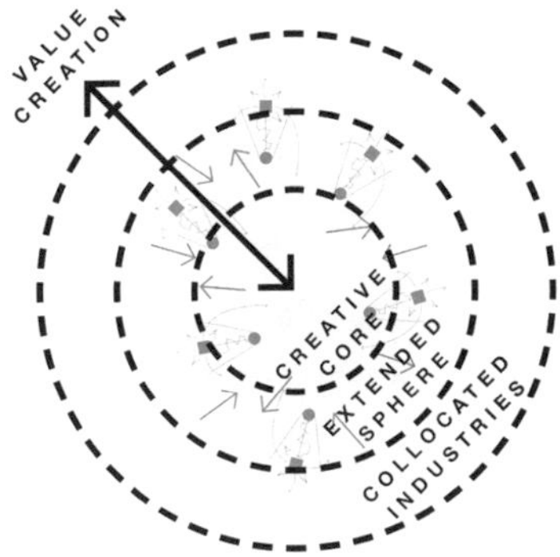

Fig. 3

and Sports (DCMS) with its 11 submarkets? How should we deal with research labs or think tanks, which are not part of this definition? Would it be appropriate to use a broader term that includes them, such as *creative economies*?
Let us investigate whether zooming out could mean something apart from zooming away or reducing complexity.
Let us see if we can zoom out and increase complexity at the same time.
We might think of a designer working on a gamification strategy for a bank's new customer generation. He works closely with a software developer and the client is the Swiss Banking Association. Or we might think of a pharmaceutical lab doing research on portable x-ray equipment. The lab collaborates intensively with entrepreneurship specialists who are developing an accurate business model for the client, which is a UN agency.
Creative Economies are situated in fields of action involving a *creative core* of original creation, an *extended sphere* of creative and innovative actors, and a multitude of *collo cated organizations and industries* (see fig. 3). This creative core only exists if there is an extended sphere and collocated areas – and vice versa. Scaling up and scaling down are interdependent or even simultaneous (as we have seen, there

is no zooming out without zooming in). It is therefore not surprising that the value creation of the creative economies stretches across all three spheres.

Value creation is characterized by process constellations that constantly interlink creation, development, realization, production, dissemination, staging, knowledge development, communication, and archiving in new ways. This is already common knowledge. Due to important influences of digitization or due to the influences of shifts from producer to consumer, there are fewer and fewer linear mechanisms. Moreover, by zooming in further we realize an interesting phenomenon. Important zones of value creation seem to be the areas of transition between creative core, the extended sphere and the collocated industries.

Again, we need a closer look at these areas. On this note, this is the right moment to listen to Simon's voice again.

(5) Fourth Part: From Culture Management to Curatorial Entrepreneurship

Thank you, Christoph. In order to be operative within and across the different spheres of the creative economies, as well as to deal with the inherent uncertainties implied in creative alternatives to the world we know, traditional approaches to management do not really work. As a consequence, we have to explore which organizing practices and processes enable and foster entrepreneurial initiatives in the creative economies. Here we can identify four important patterns (see fig. 4):

A: Organizing and strategizing in the creative economies is about *staging stories*: it is about coordinating, integrating and relating, not through managerial intervention, but through telling and materializing interesting projections through narrating worlds as they could be.

B: The world as it is and as we know it can only be productively challenged and changed if the modes through which we value things can be changed at the same time: we need

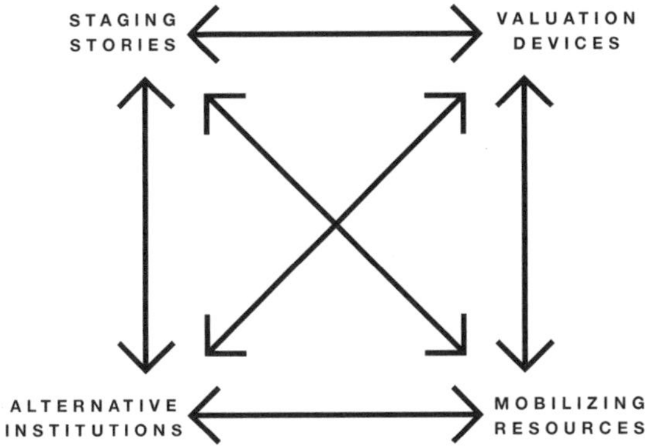

Fig. 4

alternative *valuation devices* that make a difference and render this difference tangible. We are familiar with a series of such devices, including rankings, evaluations, assessments, measurements, exhibitions, and so on: we argue that reinventing them leads to a complete reframing of what is valued, and thus of what is possible.
C: In order to make such reframing happen, *resource mobilization* becomes fundamental to be able to attract, generate and allocate the necessary financial and nonfinancial resources for making things happen and to build and establish alternative judgement devices: what is needed and needs to be mobilized are money and expertise, trust and attention, accomplices and partners, technologies and institutions.
D: In many cases, however, this does not work sustainably within existing institutions (universities, museums, corporations, offices, internet platforms, distribution channels, and so on), but requires the creation of *alternative institutions* that provide the contexts, platforms and formats for exploring such alternatives as well as realizing them in the form of novel formats for exhibitions and performances, unconventional forms of enterprises and experimental projects.

Taken together, these important patterns and practices can be identified as a promising alternative to leadership and management: *curating* – understood in a very specific sense, far removed from the everyday use we observe, for example, in marketing contexts. It is the curatorial approach – working with the dynamics of zooming in and zooming out, of protecting or exposing, of projecting and narrating – that enables scaling in new ways, beyond established institutions and settings.
How far this can go becomes visible (and remains to a large extent invisible) in a very important recent movement, whose long-term impact and relevance we cannot yet understand: the umbrella movement in Hong Kong. This is the end of our exploration, and maybe the beginning of an alternative future."

(6) Closing

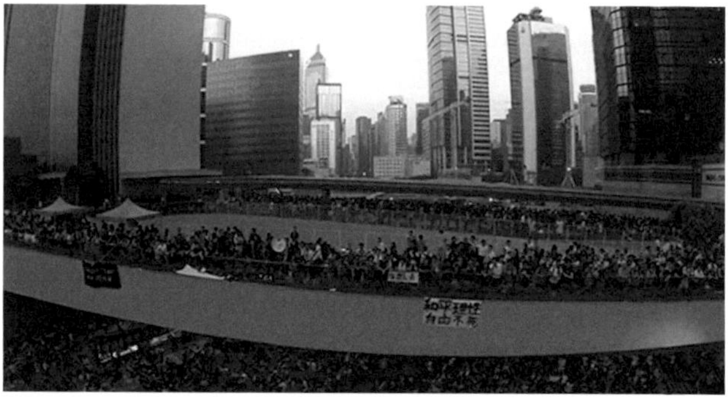

Video still 2 (Curating can bring about alternative institutionalizations: The umbrella movement occupying the central area of Hong Kong in fall 2014: © Nero Chan)
Source: Drone Shows Thousands Filling Hong Kong Streets, *online at: www.youtube.com/watch?v=vPvxvOWQJl4 (accessed 26 September 2016)*

(7) Reflection on the Setting: Palaver Revisited

Presenting in a palaver setting implies a disconnection of visual presentation, voices, speakers and audiences. As a consequence, the typical close interactive connection between the speaker(s) and the audience achieved through a traditional format no longer works. This leads to a much more loosely coupled constellation, modularizing the different elements of an academic talk, but eventually opening up new possibilities and connections. At the same time, the visual aspect of the presentation becomes more relevant. The sketches are an experiment in defining a new visual language that allows us to discuss the complex topic of the creative economies with a wider audience.

References

Boltanski, Luc, and Eve Chiapello, 1999, *Le nouvel esprit du capitalisme*. Paris: Gallimard.

Düllo, Thomas, and Franz Liebl, 2005, *Cultural Hacking: Kunst des Strategischen Handelns*. Wien: Springer.

Grand, Simon, and Wolfgang Jonas, 2012, *Mapping Design Research*. Basel: Birkhäuser.

Hess, Charlotte, and Elinor Ostrom, 2007, *Understanding Knowledge as a Commons*. Cambridge, MA: MIT Press.

Karpik, Lucien, 2010, *Valuing the Unique: The Economics of Singularities*. Princeton: Princeton University Press.

Langley, Ann, 1999, 'Strategies for Theorizing from Process Data' in *Academy of Management Review* 24(4): 691–710.

Lessing, Lawrence, 1999, 'The Law of the Horse: What Cyberlaw Might Teach' in *Harvard Law Review* 113(2): 23–38.

Maeda, John, 2004, *Simplicity*. Cambridge, MA: MIT Press.

Martel, Frédéric, 2010, *Mainstream: Enquête sur la guerre globale de la culture et des médias*. Paris: Flammarion.

Reckwitz, Andreas, 2012, *Die Erfindung der Kreativität: Zum Prozess gesellschaftlicher Ästhetisierung*. Frankfurt a.M.: Suhrkamp.

Shifman, Limor, 2014, *Meme: Kunst, Kultur und Politik im digitalen Zeitalter*. Frankfurt a.M.: Suhrkamp.

Spinosa, Charles, Fernando Flores and Hubert L. Dreyfus, 2001, *Disclosing New Worlds: Entrepreneurship, Democratic Action, and the Cultivation of Solidarity*. Cambridge, MA: MIT Press.

Sutton, Robert I., and Huggy Rao, 2014, *Scaling Up Excellence: Getting to More without Settling for Less*. London: Random House Business Books.

Toma, Yann, and Rose Marie Barrientos, 2008, *Les entreprises critiques. Critical companies*. Paris: CERAP Editions.

Von Gehlen, Dirk, 2011, *Mashup: Lob der Kopie*. Frankfurt a.M.: Suhrkamp.

Simon Grand (*1968, Zurich) is strategy designer and knowledge entrepreneur, founder and head of the RISE Management Innovation Lab and professor of strategic management at the University of St. Gallen, research fellow at the Zurich University of the Arts and co-curator of the research venture CreativeEconomies.

Christoph Weckerle is Director of the Department of Cultural Analysis at the Zurich University of the Arts. He is a cultural policy researcher and was awarded the Swiss Design Prize for his research in the field of creative economies. Weckerle is co-curator of the research venture Creative-Economies.

More information: www.creativeeconomies.com

Adrien Lucca

The Reproduction of Colours as a Process of Scaling Light Intensity

Adrien Lucca

The Reproduction of Colours as a Process of Scaling Light Intensity

This article examines the relationship between colours, mathematical representations of physical light stimuli, and the reproduction of such stimuli following the rules of colorimetry that define my artistic practice historically and at present. This context is presented in relation to a process of scaling that lies at the heart of the algorithms that I used in my recent artist's publication *Album Source* (2015).

I refer to the following definition of the verb *scaling*: "to alter [a quantity or property] by changing the units in which it is measured; to change the size of [a system or device] while keeping its parts in constant proportion" (Simpson 1989). Scaling refers to a change of symbols, units, or to a *proportional transformation* of the physical quantities of space, time, or energy. For example, we can describe a photographic print as a device that uses pigments which reflect ambient light to reproduce the visual values of an original scene – under which form and by which means the original scene existed is irrelevant here. By scaling down the luminous intensity relations present in an original scene, a photographic print generates another light field. It is an *alteration*, as in most cases a photograph does not reproduce the original light but presents an approximation of its visual appearance.[1] We will see that it is unfortunate but true that light and colour

1 One exception is the Lippmann photographic process, where the photographic plate physically records the actual wavelengths of the light field from a given point of view using a common lens. Information on Gabriel Lippmann's colour photography process can be found on the official website of the Nobel Prize (Biedermann 2005).

can be recorded and measured much more accurately than they can be reproduced by artistic media such as painting, printing, or even most digital displays.[2]

Album Source and colorimetry

Album Source (Lucca 2015) is a small-format collection of prints in a limited edition of three that presents how I combined spectrophotometry, computer programming and an inkjet printer to 'paint'. It was originally designed as a modified and portable version of a previous exhibition[3] and as an attempt to present the process of the construction of my recent artworks. It is also a prototype for a future, larger edition. The album has been on display in several art exhibitions and art fairs in 2015 and 2016.[4] It is composed of a cardboard folder containing a text and 9 inkjet prints.

This work is based on an explicitly chosen combination of scientific methodology and visual art that has formed the centre of my artistic practice over the last few years. I explore the physical limits of my inkjet printer,[5] make use of mathematical representations of light, and use computer programming and the scientific models of colorimetry[6] in order to create computer-generated printed pictures. The whole process presents similarities with a photographic process: each picture represents the light field of an original scene with extreme accuracy by the means of precision instruments, but the original light field is virtual and no camera is used. The print series is also 'site-specific' to my particular printer in the sense that it is a study – almost like a 'demo' – of what this machine does and what it can do with the help of my methodology.

The beginning of the album is a study of the machine's colour capabilities: sheet *a* is a palette of 1728 colours that covers the printer's whole colour space.[7] It has been printed separately first and used to measure every

2 A way of obtaining higher spectral purity levels is to simply illuminate paints with coloured lights. However, if the coloured light also illuminates the surroundings, the visual effect of spectrally pure stimuli is diminished or lost because of the chromatic adaptation of our visual system. After spending some time in a room illuminated by a red lamp, we can no longer see things coloured red.

3 Adrien Lucca, 'Colorimetric Pictures, C-Box – La Centrale Electrique', September 2015, Brussels.

4 Most notably in the contemporary art museum IKOB, Eupen, Belgium.

5 The physical limits explored here are the colorimetric limits on a given media, the specialized matte inkjet canvas produced by Canson.

6 "Standards" on International Commission on Illumination (CIE) website. Online at http://www.cie.co.at/index.php/Publications/Standards (accessed 26 September 2016).

7 This is similar to the coloured pictures that are used to generate ICC profiles in the graphics industry.

colour patch with a spectrophotometer. This set of measurements constitutes something like the printer's unique 'id card'. The sheets *b* and *c* are two representations of this unique colour space in a diagram where all possible colours can be represented.[8] Seen in three dimensions in an isometric perspective from the top and the bottom, the colour space looks like a triangular potato-shaped hull with five vertices that are white, red, green, blue and black. The surface of this hull defines, for this specific printing medium, the absolute limits of the printer's colours in every hue and lightness when the print is illuminated by a standard 'daylight' source.[9]

Colour is not light (i.e. visible electromagnetic energy). It is not a property of the material substances around us, nor a stimulation of the retina, nor a property of light. However, the visual appearance of a colour is predetermined by the type and intensity of the light that is transformed by material substances, which ends up in our eyes stimulating the retina. Colours are sensations synthesized in our brains, and we cannot measure the effect of light stimulation of the retina directly in the brain cells.

Modern colorimetry was standardized in 1931[10] as a way to link sensations of colour with existing physical units that characterize light, and as a way to measure, encode, and when possible help to reproduce any colour in a system based on three well-defined primary coloured lights – red, green and blue-violet (RGB[11]). In short, colorimetry does not say anything about the physical quantities behind an existing colour stimulus, it only defines three quantities X, Y, Z of RGB lights that, once added together, produce an equivalent stimulus. In other words, colorimetry allows the calculation of RGB intensities necessary for the composition of a light stimulus

8 "8.1 CIE 1976 uniform chromaticity scale diagram (UCS diagram)" in Carter (2004: 16).

9 "Table T.1. Relative spectral power distributions of CIE illuminants" (Carter 2004: 30–32). The data was originally published in "CIE-15.2-1986 table 1.1 Part 2: CIE Standard illuminant D65 relative spectral power distribution 300 nm–830 nm at 5 nm intervals" in *CIE 15: Technical Report: Colorimetry, 2nd edition*, 1986. Online at: http://www.cie.co.at/publ/abst/datatables15_2004/sid65.txt (accessed 26 September 2016).

10 For an exhaustive history of CIE colorimetry, see Janós Scanda (2005).

11 There are many RGB systems defined by their reference white, their primary colours, and by their intended use. The original CIE RGB used three monochromatic primaries at standardized wavelengths of 700 nm (red), 546.1 nm (green) and 435.8 nm (blue), and the RGB values correspond to linear variations of the light sources' intensities – for many other RGB colour systems this is not the case, and a non-linear transformation (usually named the 'gamma') is applied on the values. Non-linear RGB systems are intended for computer screen displays (e.g. sRGB) or for digital photography (e.g. Adobe RGB (98), ProPhoto RGB, Adobe Wide Gamut RGB); their non-linearity allows finer variations in the dark values, where the eyes are the most sensitive, and higher levels of data compression. Useful data can be found in Bruce Lindbloom, *RGB Working Space Information*. Online at http://www.brucelindbloom.com/index.html?WorkingSpaceInfo.html (accessed 26 September 2016).

S2 that is visually equivalent to a stimulus *S1* defined by a measured light spectrum also called a Spectral Power Distribution (SPD in colorimetric jargon). The intensities of RGB primaries that match the original stimulus define three coordinates in a colour space (one value for each primary R, G, B or X, Y, Z). And these three values are the colour measurement itself.

The colorimetric system published by the Commission Internationale de l'Éclairage (CIE) in 1931 and its more recent updates allow the characterization of light sources and colours and the calculation of their additive mixtures in a way that 19th-century scientists, colour theorists, photographers, or painters who had a strong interest in colour theory (like Georges Seurat) could only dream of. Strangely enough – possibly because of its physico-mathematical nature – the success and the understanding of CIE colorimetry in the artistic world has long been very poor or nonexistent, even though today every single user of Adobe Photoshop and other popular software performs complex colour transformations that rely on it.

The standard observer

The standard observer tables, or colour matching functions (CMFs), are the result of colour matching experiments performed independently by William David Wright and John Guild in the 1920s–30s, with a total of 17 human observers (Shaw and Fairchild s.a.: 3). The creation of this tool marked a peak in the development of the theory of trichromacy that started in the 19th century when scientists like Young, Maxwell, Helmholtz, Graßmann and others built a theory stating that all colours can be described as variations of three parameters.[12] The standard observer is the cornerstone of the colorimetric system. It represents an average human retina's reaction to a stimulus by individual wavelengths across the visible electromagnetic spectrum.[13] It is a table of numerical values containing RGB colour matching values for each wavelength. Thanks to these empirically derived functions – the averaged physiological reaction of 17 human observers to a set of light stimuli – any physical stimulus can be transformed into a colorimetric measurement.

12 James Clerck Maxwell's theory of colour vision in particular is seen by historians as the origin of colorimetry, see Narciso Silverstrini (1994).

13 The standard observer represents an average individual who sees colours "normally", i.e., is not colour-blind. It is also possible to create similar functions for each type of colour blindness (cf. Shaw and Fairchild s.a.: 3).

The colour matching experiment links physical quantities of light with the retinal responses of a human observer under daylight conditions, given a specified central angle of vision of 2° or 10°.[14] In this central region, the retina responds to light stimuli through the activity of three types of cells: the S, M, L cones are highly sensitive to electromagnetic radiation of short, medium and long wavelengths within a window of approximately one "octave" of electromagnetic radiation (mostly between 400 and 700 nanometres). The retina cells do not separate individual wavelengths. Remarkably, a very large number of different physical light spectra produce the same reaction, generating identical colour sensations. Different physical stimuli that generate identical colour sensations are called *metameric*. For instance, a large number of combinations of two monochromatic lights of complementary wavelengths can synthesize identical sensations of white. Colour metamerism is the condition that allows any colour sensation to be translated into RGB values in a colour matching experiment.

Some of the best quality data used in today's colour measurement devices and algorithms[15] are the data behind the *CIE 1964 10° standard observer*. They are based on the average physiological reaction to light stimuli of 49 human individuals of diverse ages and genders.[16] Even today, any light stimuli can be coded as RGB equivalents because the eye-print of 49 now dead or elderly people still continues to function.[17]

Painting and printing light

The next six sheets of my publication *Album Source* are attempts at 'printing visual equivalents of light objects' within the limits of the colour space specified by the physical and colorimetric measurements of the data from the first section. The palette of 1728 colours printed on sheet *a* defines what colorimetrists call the *gamut* of a printing device that determines the range of colours available to print pictures.

14 Details about the construction of CMFs can be found on the "Colour matching functions" webpage of the Colour & Vision Research Laboratory (CVRL), London. Online at http://cvrl.ioo.ucl.ac.uk/database/text/intros/introcmfs.htm (accessed 26 September 2016). The CVRL also provides numerical data for CMFs online at http://cvrl.ioo.ucl.ac.uk/cmfs.htm and data concerning the spectral sensitivities of protanopia and deuteranopia, two common kinds of colour blindness online at http://cvrl.ioo.ucl.ac.uk/dimono.htm (accessed 26 September 2016).

15 The Stiles-Burch 10 deg RGB CMFs (1959).

16 The complete data is available as an Excel file on the CVRL website. Online at http://cvrl.ioo.ucl.ac.uk/database/data/sb_individual/SB10_corrected_indiv_CMFs.xls (accessed 26 September 2016).

17 Most software still uses the second standard observer from 1931 for historical and compatibility reasons.

Using this scientific approach, my work connects itself to the history of Western painting. In particular, I trace a trans-generational project in this history that consists of 'painting the light'. I believe that a lot of time, energy, money, and grey matter has been spent by Western artists ever since the Middle Ages[18] on studying, painting, and magnifying the appearance of light. This project existed long before colorimetry was standardized by the CIE and before photography was invented. Using the visual values of pigments under light, some painters tried to reproduce light and colours as they appear in the real world. This is at least what any 'optically realistic' painting seems to do. Works by the tenebrists La Tour and de Coster point out what I call the fundamental problem of 'figuration of light in material pictures'. This problem is not limited to the field of painting, as it appears in colour photography as well.

If one takes a closer look at the idea of painting light, there are many arguments in favour of its impossibility and absurdity. First of all, there is no defined limit to the intensity of light in the real world. A contrast ratio of 1:100,000 in an outdoor scene is common (Freeman and Durand s.a.), while in tempera painting techniques, for example, the contrast between the whitest and the blackest pigments (titanium white PW6 and iron-manganese spinel black PBk26) reaches only a ratio of ± 1:40. High-end inkjet printers produce similar results on matte media and go as far as ± 1:100 on glossy photo paper. Varnished oil paintings can yield slightly better contrast ratios, but are still many orders of magnitude behind outdoor scenes. Even the contrast between *Vantablack* (the super black material for which Anish Kapoor recently acquired exclusive rights[19]) and *Spectralon* (the whitest existing reflective non-fluorescent material) will not go beyond ± 1:3000.

In a painting, the colour gamut is determined by the optical properties of the pigments used. Their colour is caused by the absorption of some parts of the light spectrum. However, no pigment ever absorbs 100 % of any part of the light spectrum, just like no black paint absorbs all light. A deep

18 In my opinion this interest in the study of light originates in religious beliefs and the early scientific study of nature. As examples from early times, we might mention the *theology of light* of Abbot Suger of Saint-Denis (1081–1151), the very precise representation of light effects in the paintings of Jan van Eyck (c. 1390–1441): glass, pearls, metals, hairs..., the *divine light* in the paintings of Fra Angelico (1395–1455) or the *atmospheric perspective* of Leonardo da Vinci (1452–1519).

19 Cf. for example online at http://www.lemonde.fr/arts/article/2016/03/03/anish-kapoor-se-paie-le-noir-parfait_4875569_1655012.html (accessed 26 September 2016).

hole that traps light usually appears darker than existing black substances. On the other hand, it is easy to understand that pigments never reflect more than the incoming light, but always at least a little bit less.[20] Regarding the colourfulness of pigments versus natural light phenomena, the following example will make aspiring neo-impressionists aware of the difficulty of their task: even the most colourful available orange pigment (probably DPP Orange, PO73, a modern pigment which was not available at the time of the neo-impressionists) emits a less orange light illuminated by noon sunlight than the light reflected by a piece of white paper at sunset when sunlight has precisely the same hue as the DPP Orange. Colours that are born from reflections of light by material substances have well-known and impassable limits.[21]

This shows that scaling down natural optical phenomena is not always possible. If we want to paint an optical or a colorimetric 'copy' of this white paper as it is illuminated at sunset we will encounter unsolvable problems: pigments will turn out to be either too dark, not colourful enough, or both. There is no way to create a metameric combination of the yellows, oranges, reds and pinks that a nice sunset offers with paints. Among the coloured materials used by artists, only coloured glass can match the purity of a sunset's colours because the physical process by which the colour is produced – not by reflection but by *transmission* of light through coloured glass – allows much higher spectral purity levels.[22]

Star's light

Sheet *f* of the *Album Source*, titled: *Star's light – D65 neutral White, contrast 1:33, distance to the surface: 3.75 centimetres* (fig. 1) illustrates well the problem of the figuration of light and how it is related to the limited contrast ratio of the media. In this picture I wanted to print an exact visual equivalent of the light that a punctual and omnidirectional light source

20 Fluorescent pigments seem to reflect more visible light because they convert invisible energy (ultraviolet radiation) into visible energy. Unfortunately, most fluorescent materials are not lightfast. We are currently studying a new material that could change the game: quantum dots. But the current price of this material – used in biology to mark proteins in living cells – is prohibitive (about 6000 € per gram), and it is a serious hazard.

21 These limits are called MacAdam limits, after the name of the colour scientist who first defined them theoretically. Other researchers – in particular Michael Pointer – have tried to define these limits by collecting thousands of coloured natural and artificial material samples (cf. Pointer 1980).

22 We are currently working with similar methods on a stained-glass project that involves the reproduction of sunset colours for a permanent installation in the metro station Place d'Armes in Montreal, QC, Canada.

(a 'microscopic star') projects on a white screen situated in a dark room. Mathematically speaking, this situation can be represented in a 3D space by a point "O" that emits similar light in every direction, and by a plane "P" that cuts the spherical emission. The intensity of the light that reaches any point "p" on the plane depends on the inverse of the square of the distance [Op] that separates the two points.

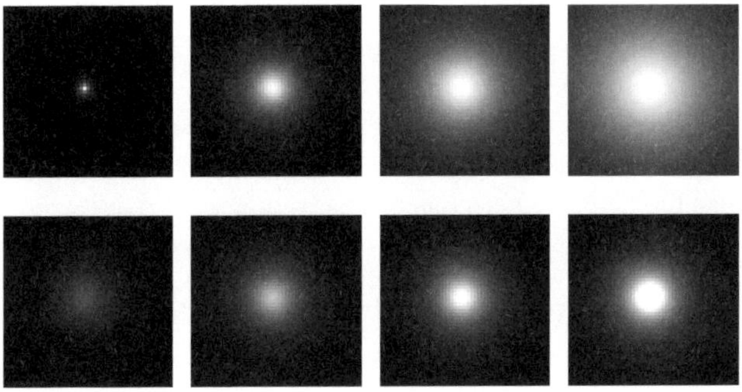

Fig.1 Results of the variation of two parameters: (Top) variation of the distance between the star and the screen. The closer the light source is to the screen, the smaller the light imprint and the higher the contrast ratio of the picture. In the bottom row we see the variation of the star's emission intensity. In the above row at a certain level of intensity the centre of the picture becomes white, like in the case of over-exposure in photography, and the data is lost.

The darkness of the black and the lightness of the white available predetermine the limits within which making an image of light, an image generated by a mathematical model, is possible. *Intensity scaling* becomes a necessity: the distance between the star, the projection plane, and the intensity of the light that the virtual star emits can all be used as adjustment variables to produce an 'optimal' picture. The centre of this picture is as light as possible and the corners as dark as possible.

In *Star's Light*, the centre ended up 33 times lighter than the corners (the contrast ratio is equal to 1:33). Colorimetric calculations that control the choice of the colour of every pixel of the picture produced a printed surface that reflects ambient light according to the model. This light acts as a visual equivalent of a light gradient that a punctual light source situated at 3.55 cm from the centre of the picture would have produced on a white screen in a dark room.

Scaling light intensity within the available dynamic range: difficulties and solutions

When we look at the history of painting from the perspective of the figuration of light, we can interpret some paintings as attempts at solving it. *Mary Magdalene with a Night Light* (c. 1640, Musée du Louvre, fig. 2) by Georges de La Tour (1593–1652) is a tenebrist-style painting in the spirit of the followers of Caravaggio. As beautifully as this picture depicts its subject, from a strictly optical point of view there is something 'illegal' happening with the flame of the candle: the flame is not bright enough. Flames in dark rooms belong to a group of objects that cannot be painted realistically[23] because no pigment under ambient light will ever emit sufficient light to produce an effect on our eyes that compares with the effect of a real flame in the dark. Apart from being 'illegal', the decision to put the light source in the picture also has an obvious technical disadvantage: the painter has to restrict his use of the lightest pigments to the flame itself, which means that the rest of the picture will be depicted one grade darker than otherwise: the presence of the light source inside the picture limits the possibilities of modulating lights and shadows in the rest of the picture (if the flame was painted with the same lightness as, say, the skin of Mary, we would immediately notice that something is wrong).

A most beautiful solution can be found to the problem of the flame. About five years later, in *Joseph the Carpenter* (1645, Musée du Louvre, see detail in fig. 3), also by La Tour – or in *A Man Singing by Candlelight* (1625–1635, National Gallery of Ireland, fig. 4), an earlier work by the Flemish painter Adam de Coster (c. 1586–1643), the light source is still placed within the scene, but is hidden by an object. The object is the hand of Jesus Christ depicted as a child in La Tour, or a songbook represented as a deep stripe of black shadow in de Coster's painting – where it almost seems that part of the picture is missing! Solving the flame problem opens up more possibilities for colour modulation in the rest of the picture. For instance, while the light still comes "from within the picture" – suggesting an intimate space around it – the skin of the child's face can now be as bright as the flame was in the previous example, and the same is true for the costume of the singing man, in particular his white collar and his belt.

23 This group also includes embers (reason A: the colour is too spectrally pure), the sun (reason B: usually too bright), some rainbows (reason A), the bottom part of a CD or DVD-ROM (reasons A & B), light dispersed by a prism in a dark room (reason A), laser light (reason A).

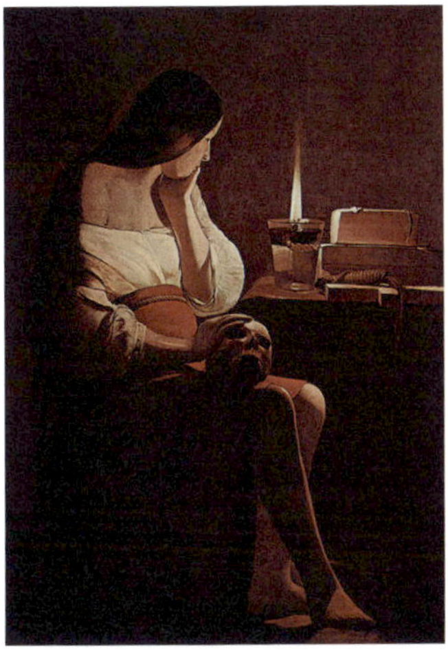

Fig. 2

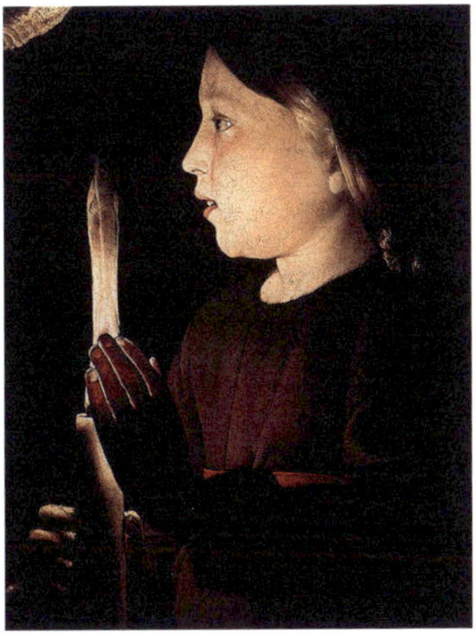

Fig. 3

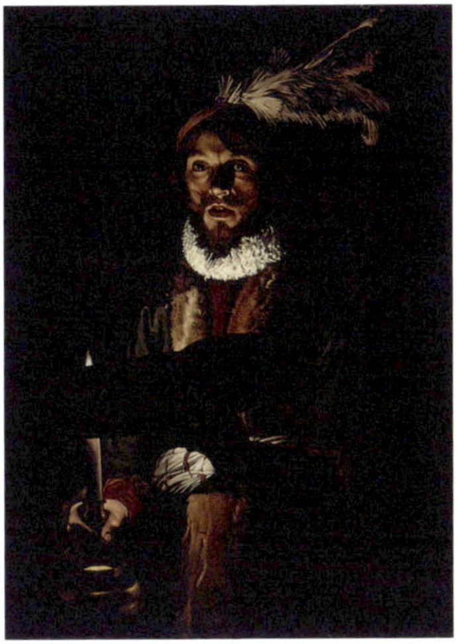

Fig.4

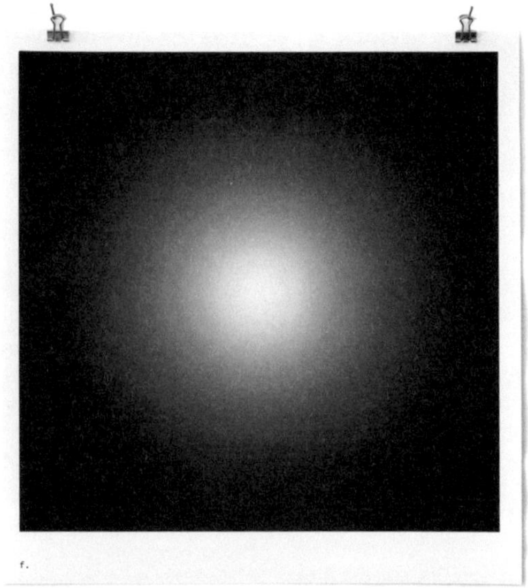

Fig. 5

'Manips' and figuration

In La Tour's *Joseph the Carpenter*, the light has a double existence as a terrestrial and artificial (man-made) phenomenon: a candle, and a metaphysical existence as part of the trinity: Joseph representing the Father, Jesus the Son, and light representing the Holy Ghost.

In a materialistic sense, the picture was fabricated as a device that reproduces the visual sensation of an otherwise missing light source, an object that acts in the physical world as a 'parasite' using the energy of the ambient light to appear to the beholders' eyes. However, while this definition seems to apply, and even though this might have been the painter's intention, the painting depicts more than only the illusion of the sensation of light.

The pictures of *Album Source* also act as physical 'light parasites', but their nature is much closer to what French scientists call a 'manip',[24] which stands for the material part of a scientific experiment, that is, the test itself. This expression implies that a result has been foreseen by a scientific theory that the manip will verify. *Album Source* as a whole is a series of

24 This expression is the short version of the French scientific term *manipulation*.

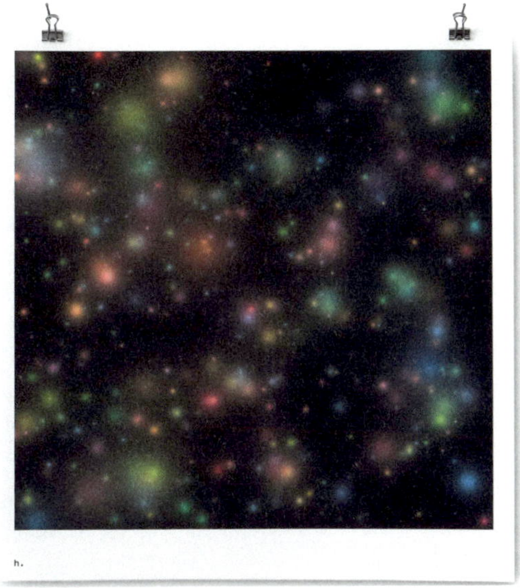

Fig. 6: AP 1/3 of the edition of 10+3AP High density *(2015), 60 x 64 cm unique inkjet print on canvas.*

such manips, a journey within the possibilities opened up by the logic of colorimetry and the existence of precision inkjet printers.

However, this difference between theory and experiment does not mean that the game is over: the light also has a double existence as the visual presence of something absent. In fact, this is the subject matter of the picture: the apparition of a light imprint in a painting-like space, the light source being unseen because it is off-screen. As hard as I try, I can never affirm that such a picture is non-figurative, because the manip itself aims at reproducing the model of something that could perfectly well exist. That is also probably a reason why the picture really *seems to be* a light imprint. *Star's Light* is a visually equivalent picture of the physical situation that we have modelled mathematically *in virtuo*.

Clouds of stars

The three last sheets of *Album Source* are pictures generated by an algorithm that superimposes several light sources on the same surface. *Maquette v.0.2.5*, sheet *h* of the album, is a composition made of a predefined number of coloured lights. The colour, distance, and horizontal and vertical positions of each light were randomized within predefined limits with a pseudorandom number generator.[25] The resulting pictures irresistibly evoke constellations, nebulae, or galaxies as captured by the Hubble and other telescopes since 1990. The famous *Hubble Deep Field* and *Hubble Ultra Deep Field* were definitely a source of inspiration.[26] However, in reality the pictures are a well-tuned small virtual light play, optimally rendered by the printer's pigments as visual equivalents on high quality printing media with the help of colorimetry. The technique we have developed can produce very light or very colourful pictures that give the impression of actually emitting light.

In May and July 2015, I introduced two new versions of this algorithm: v.0.2.7 "Spectre paramétrique" (French for 'parametric spectrum') and v.0.2.8 "High density" (fig. 6).

Conclusion

Using examples from the history of Western painting, tenebrist painting of the Baroque period in particular, I have shown that the problem of the figuration of light was tackled by artists long before I approached it.

I have tried to present to the reader my methodology, in which the reproduction of colours allowed by the scientific tools provided by CIE colorimetry can be used to print visual equivalents of the effects of light sources. This methodology entails the making of a model of light using physical properties (intensity, diffusion across space, and spectrum), a numerical process to scale and optimize the digital values to adapt them to the extent of the colour space available to us, and a precision instrument to produce images.

25 There are two main approaches to generating random numbers using a computer: pseudorandom number generators (PRNGs) and true random number generators (TRNGs). For an introduction to random numbers and randomness, and their usage in the sciences and arts see 'What's this fuss about *true* randomness?', online at https://www.random.org/#numbers (accessed 26 September 2016).

26 I was 7 years old in 1990 and like many other kids I was fascinated by the pictures of the outer space. Only recently I have realized how revolutionary the Hubble telescope pictures that I grew up watching were: "No telescope before Hubble had the resolution to see these distant galaxies. Intrigued, astronomers turned Hubble on what appeared to be a nearly empty patch of sky and let it soak up all the light it could for ten days [18 to 28 Dec. 1995]. They were taking a risk – most Hubble observations take just hours, and the time being eaten up could have been used for more concrete needs. It was possible the objects the astronomers were looking for would be too faint or small for even Hubble to see. But the results turned up a treasure trove: 3,000 galaxies, large and small, shapely and amorphous, burning in the depths of space. The stunning image was called the Hubble Deep Field." Cf. Space Telescope Science Institute, "Taking the Universe's Baby Pictures" *Breakthroughs in Cosmology*, online at http://hubblesite.org/hubble_discoveries/breakthroughs/cosmology (accessed 26 September 2016).

The extent of our colour space depends on the properties of our media – in the present case: an inkjet printer and a specialized canvas – that we have to study beforehand. The methodology that we developed applies to any media as long as we can characterize their colours and reproduce the characteristics that we measured.

I have identified two limits that cannot always be reached together: the colour saturation and the contrast ratio. The medium used determines these impassable limitations, but I warn the reader about the fact that there is no medium that does not present similar limitations. Printing or painting light is possible, but if we follow the rule of optical realism (which is only one way to achieve such a thing) we have to define these limitations in the first place before we can find new ways to overcome them.

References

Biedermann, Klaus, 2005, *Lippmann's and Gabor's Revolutionary Approach to Imaging.* Online at http://www.nobelprize.org/nobel_prizes/themes/physics/biedermann/ (accessed 26 September 2016).

Carter, E.C., et al., (International Commission on Illumination), 2004, *CIE 15: Technical Report: Colorimetry, 3rd ed.* Washington: The Federal Register. Online at http://www.cdvplus.cz/file/3-publikace-cie15-2004/ (accessed 26 September 2016).

Freeman, Bill, and Frédo Durand, s.a., 'Dynamic Range and Contrast' in *Syllabus of the course 6.098 Digital and Computational Photography and 6.882 Advanced Computational Photography* (online). Cambridge, MA: MIT/EECS URL. Online at http://groups.csail.mit.edu/graphics/classes/CompPhoto06/html/lecturenotes/08_HDR_6.pdf (accessed 26 September 2016).

Lucca, Adrien, 2015, *Maquette, Album Source Version alpha*, March 2015. Brussels: Ed. JAP.

Pointer, Michael, 1980, 'The Gamut of Real Surface Colors' in *Color Research and Application* 5: 145–155.

Schanda, Janós, 2005, *Colorimetry: Understanding the CIE System.* New York: John Wiley & Sons.

Shaw, Mark, and Mark Fairchild, s.a., *Evaluating the 1931 CIE Color Matching Functions.* Online at http://rit-mcsl.org/fairchild/PDFs/PAP11.pdf (accessed 26 September 2016).

Simpson, J.A., et.al. 1989, *The Oxford English Dictionary*, 2nd ed. Oxford: Clarendon Press.

Silvestrini, Narciso, 1994, *IdeaColour.* Zurich: Baumann & Stromer publisher. Online at http://www.colorsystem.com/?lang=en (accessed 26 September 2016).

Adrien Lucca (*1983, Paris) is an artist, independent researcher, and professor of colour theory at Ecole Nationale Supérieure des Arts Visuels de La Cambre in Brussels, Belgium. His artistic work and research focus on light, matter, their interactions and their visual appearance. Using physics, mathematics, computer programming and colorimetry, he develops artworks with various media such as painting, drawing, digital printing and stained glass. In 2016, Lucca is working on a permanent glass-light installation situated in the Place-d'Armes metro station in Montréal, Québec, Canada.

Frank Schweitzer

Limits to Scaling – and How to Move beyond Them

Frank Schweitzer
Limits to Scaling – and How to Move beyond Them

Scaling – a systemic property

Small and large systems

In engineering, the term *scaling* may be used to describe a relation between *objects* and their *models*. In the exact sciences, however, scaling is a systemic property, meaning that it relates to the system itself. Scaling describes how certain system properties change conditional on others, most notably the system size.

Taking the example of a social network, the quantity of interest could be the number of friends someone has in this social network. Then the corresponding question would be how the average number of friends scales with the size of the system, that is, the total number of members, N, of the social network. Obviously, if N is ten, then the maximum number of friends is bound to ten, and the average number should be even less. But what happens if N equals one thousand? Does the increase in the potential number of friends also lead to an increase in the *actual* number of friends? And how does this scale if N approaches ten million?

Discrete and continuous measures

The example at hand uses a *discrete* measure of system size, N. But scaling can be also applied if *continuous* measures for the system size are used, for example the volume V or the mass M of a physical system. These should be *extensive* measures, that is, they increase with system size, as opposed to *intensive* measures, which are independent of size. In fact, these extensive measures are in the limit of large numbers, for example for $N \rightarrow 10^{23}$, which is the number of atoms in one mole of a given substance, all related by simple linear transformations: $N \sim V$, where the proportionality constant is given by the particle density (which is the intensive measure), or $N \sim M$, with the molar mass of that substance as the proportionality constant.

Simple transformations

Such linear transformations are quite common in *geometric* scaling; for example, a system of length X, width Y and height Z can be scaled to a system with $X' \rightarrow aX$, $Y' \rightarrow bY$, $Z' \rightarrow cZ$. *Isotropic* scaling means that the proportionality constants a, b, c are all the same, otherwise *anisotropic* scaling is observed. If these constants are larger than 1, the system is *enlarged* (or *stretched*), otherwise the system is *contracted*.

Interesting transformations can be observed if some constants are larger and others are less than, or equal to, 1, or if instead of constants *functions* are used. An example of a *linear function*, also known as *shear mapping*, would be $X' \rightarrow aX+bY+cZ$. The famous biologist D'Arcy Wentworth Thompson used such transformations in his book *On Growth and Form (1917)* to describe the body shape of certain related biological species. An example of a *non-linear function* would be $X' \rightarrow (aX)^2\ (bY)$.

The discussion of such transformations, or *deformations*, is mostly restricted to the geometric shape of a system. Instead, we are interested in a very different question, namely how system properties change with the *size of the system*. To refer again to the physical system: is it possible that a very different system behaviour, such as a phase transition from vapour to water, can be induced/prevented if we change only the *size* of the system and keep everything else constant?

No scaling – but a natural scale

Certain systems are characterized by a natural scale that remains the same even if the system size increases. For example, the average number of offspring per human remains roughly the same irrespective of the size of the system (i.e. the number of mating options). Such systems are often described by the so-called normal distribution, $P(x) \sim N(\mu,\sigma^2)$, where the location parameter μ is given by the mean value (e.g. the average number of offspring) and σ^2 characterizes the variance. In statistics, the latter is often denoted as the scale parameter, as it describes how spread out the distribution is. For normal distributions, we expect only relatively small deviations from the mean. To put this plainly: systems with natural scales are highly predictable with respect to that scale, or quantity.

No natural scale – but scale-free

Other systems are scale-free in the sense that no characteristic scale exists. To take an example from social communication: what is the typical time interval x at which we reply to a mobile phone call, a post in a chat, a written letter? There is no such typical time lapse. Instead, we find that any possible value x, from minutes to months, occurs with a well-defined frequency that is described by a so-called scale-free distribution, also referred to as a power law, $P(x) \sim x^{-\gamma}$. Scale-free refers to the fact that if we replaced x by cx, where c is a scaling constant, that is, if we measured x in days instead of seconds, we would still have $P(cx) \sim x^{-\gamma}$. Only the proportionality factor is different and now involves the constant $c^{-\gamma}$. Hence, the distribution $P(x)$ is scale invariant. It depends on only one parameter, the scaling exponent γ, to determine how often a certain value x appears.

Remarkably, for human communication this exponent is $\gamma = 1.5$, irrespective of whether we analyse communication in chat rooms, over mobile phones, or the correspondence of Darwin or Einstein. Hence, this scale-free distribution captures the very essence of our human communicative behaviour. Depending on the value of γ, sometimes not even a mean value μ or a variance σ^2 is defined. In plain words: in scale-free systems, even rare events can occur with a non-negligible probability.

Not scale-free, but very broad

In most real cases, the distribution that determines how often a certain value appears is not exactly scale-free, but very broad. To take an example from scientometrics: how often is a scientific publication cited within a ten-year period? The number of citations has no typical value. Most publications never get cited, while a rather small number of publications gets cited several thousand times.

The frequency of a given number of citations follows a *log-normal distribution*, which looks very skewed, like a power-law, for large numbers of citations, but like a normal distribution for very small numbers of citations. In particular, it still has a defined mean value μ and variance σ^2. The citations of publications in *different scientific disciplines* all follow a log-normal distribution; however, they do not follow the same log-normal distribution. Instead, their characteristic values μ and σ^2 depend on the discipline and indirectly also on the *size*, that is, the number of publications in that discipline.

Scaling the distribution

Interestingly, we can rescale these citation distributions. In other words, we divide the number of

A fundamental difference

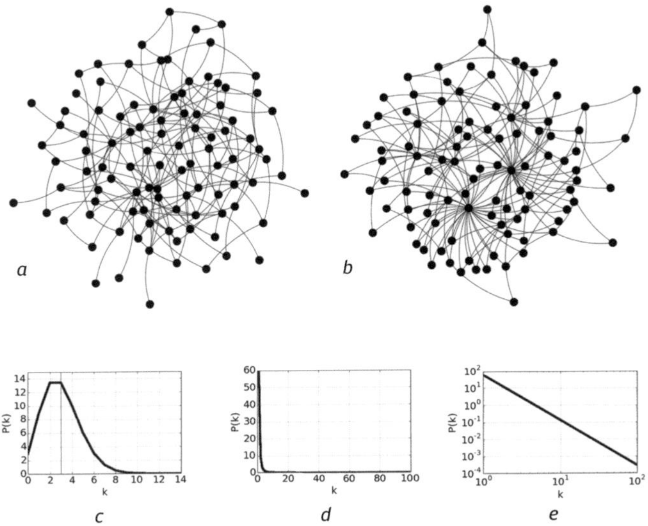

Networks (a) and (b) each consist of $N = 100$ *nodes representing users and links depicting their interactions. While the networks seem to be similar at first glance, they are very different with respect to the number of links, denoted as* degree k*, of each user. The degree distribution* $P(k)$ *gives us the frequency of finding a given degree* k *in the network. Network (a) is a so-called* random *network characterized by a Poisson distribution* $P(k)$*, shown in (c), which for large networks converges to the normal distribution* $N(\mu,\sigma^2)$*. Accordingly, the degree distribution has a well-defined mean, 3 in this case, and a rather small variance. This would not change if we considered* $N = 10.000$*, that is, the mean degree would still be 3, while outliers may have 10 or so. Network (b), on the other hand, is a so-called* scale-free *network characterized by a power law distribution* $P(k) \sim k^{-\gamma}$*. It is shown in (d), using the same linear scale as in (c) to allow comparison, and in (e) using a log-log scale. The straight line in (e) indicates that there is a non-negligible probability of finding few users with a very large degree. Hence, if we increase the network to* $N = 10.000$*, we see a larger number of users with degrees much larger than 3, maybe with degree 300 or 3000, while in (c) this probability can be safely neglected.*

citations x by the average number of citations x_0 received by all publications in that discipline published in the same year. Plotting the scaled distributions $P(x/x_0)$, we see that the log-normal distributions $P(x)$ from different disciplines all collapse into *one* master curve.

Hence, we have obtained two insights: (i) we have verified that the probability of finding a paper with a given number of citations is described by the scaled distribution $P(x/x_0)$, irrespective of scientific fields or years, and (ii) we have obtained a simple scaling function $x \rightarrow x/x_0$ that accounts for the influence of scientific disciplines via the characteristic value x_0.

The scaling function comprises two different sizes: the size of the community representing the scientific discipline and the number of publications in the respective discipline. Remarkably, these 'sizes' enter the description not directly, but indirectly. This means that the scaling function contains this information in a non-linear and highly compact manner. Finding such simple yet robust and quite universal scaling functions is one of the ultimate aims of scientific research in the exact sciences.

Scaling in input-output relations

Social and economic systems not only have their specific structure and dynamics – they also serve a purpose. This means that we can relate their performance, or output in general, to other variables, notably the system size or other input variables. To give an example from economics: if we increase the *input* of capital and labour by a factor of two, how would that impact the *output* of the system, for example, the production of some goods?

The most common case is known as *decreasing returns to scale* (DRS): if we double the input (e.g. labour), we do not get twice the output but *less* because, for example, the administrative costs for hiring and managing a larger workforce have considerably increased. DRS set limits to further growth because beyond a given production size any further increase of production is rendered *unprofitable*. The desired scenario would be *increasing returns to scale* (IRS): if we double the input, we get more than twice the output – that is, the more, the better. Economists argue a great deal about how to turn DRS into IRS.

Emergence of new systemic properties

More is different

The above considerations imply that the system properties do not change with scale other than the way defined by the scaling functions. But complex systems, such as systems consisting of a large number of strongly interacting elements (usually denoted as agents), also have the property of *emergence*. This describes the sudden occurrence of new system qualities once certain critical parameters, known as thresholds or *tipping points*, are reached.

Other common terms for this sudden occurrence are *phase transitions* or *sudden regime shifts*.

An example from physics is conductivity, which is a systemic property. A single atom has no conductivity. So, how many atoms do we need to observe something like conductivity? For mercury, one finds that conductivity emerges when the number of atoms increases from a few to up to 100. Below 10, the system has no conductivity, but above 100, its measurable value cannot be distinguished from a macroscopic bulk phase with millions of billions of atoms. In plain words: above a certain system size, the system behaves completely differently.

Critical mass?

Sometimes it is very difficult to know when this critical size is reached. Actually, it is not always the *size* that defines the threshold for the emergence of new system qualities. Quite often, it can also be the interaction strength between system elements. Weak interaction may not lead to emerging phenomena, while strong interaction does.

Many variables involved in determining the tipping point are not fixed from the outside, as boundary conditions, for example, but evolve over time with the dynamics of the system. In a growing system, the system size increases over time until a critical value is reached. However information, too, can be accumulated over time until it reaches a level that changes the systemic behaviour.

This means that we need to know not only the *critical value*, but also the *time* needed to reach this value. This is what makes it so difficult to predict the onset of emergence.

Critical slowing down/speeding up

Once a critical threshold has been reached and a phase transition or a sudden regime shift has occurred at a particular time t_c , we cannot assume that established regularities will still hold afterwards. This also implies a breakdown of scaling relations, which need to be replaced by other relations describing the new phase or regime.

Remarkably, however, the dynamics of *approaching* the tipping point of a phase transition follow their own *time-dependent* scaling laws. This is known as *critical slowing down*, but critical speeding up can also occur. It means that in the vicinity of a tipping point, the system does not behave just randomly, but shows signatures in the dynamics that indicate a coming phase transition. They often contain terms of the form $(t_c-t)^\alpha$ where the scaling exponent α can be positive or negative. For example, in ecology certain processes such as recovery occur at a much lower rate close to a tipping point than they do otherwise, whereas in economics fluctuations of prices may increase considerably when approaching tipping points.

Beyond scaling

Change the system

Distributions define the probability of a given value, while scaling functions describe how system properties change with system size or with input variables. Scaling functions allow us to predict the systemic behaviour, but on the other hand also set limits to what should be expected from a system – and what not.

However, the most interesting question, for both social and economic systems, is how to move beyond scaling. As scaling is a systemic property, this implies *changing* the system. Change, on the other hand, is a double-edged sword: social and economic systems are *adaptive systems*. This means that whatever we propose to 'improve' the system will result in the system responding in *both* intended and unintended ways. 'Unintended' is not the same as 'unforeseeable' – a systemic perspective could indeed help us to better understand the occurrence of unintended consequences. But in most cases, social and economic actors, both on the individual and the institutional level, have enough incentives *not* to adopt such a perspective.

From decreasing to increasing returns to scale

Physical production is constrained by material resources, so it naturally obeys decreasing returns to scale. This sets limits to growth and hence to profit. To vastly increase the latter, production has to be transformed to obey increasing returns to scale.

This happens in the Internet economy and is related to the *network effect*: if the size of a social network is measured by N, the number of users, we have potentially N^2 connections between all users. If we double N, we get four times more connections – if all of these connections can be utilized. Knowledge production and other forms of innovation depend crucially on such network effects.

Increasing returns to scale are also related to the production of non-rivalrous goods, that is, goods that can be possessed or used by more than one actor without their value diminishing. Examples are electronic books, music or video files and other types of information-related products that can be easily shared (and sold) without further increasing the production costs.

Hence, the digital economy can obey increasing returns to scale. However, the modern financial industry is also able to realize this. While classical stock exchange relies on a limited number of available assets that have to be possessed to be traded, derivatives are financial products that no longer require the possession of the so-called underlying product and thus allow the exponential growth of the financial market.

From decreasing to increasing attention

The number of citations is bound by the size of the scientific community that becomes aware of the respective publication, for example by browsing scientific journals. While the resource, that is, the size of the community, cannot be easily increased, the number of publications increases exponentially, which implies potentially less attention per publication.

To turn decreasing into increasing attention, one has to change the system such that new mechanisms generate more awareness for one's own publication. So scientists launch new ways of self-marketing, preferably in the social media, to popularize their work. It is then no longer the scientific quality that drives their increase in citations, it is the impact of social and mass media.

Unintended consequences

The above-mentioned changes introduce new feedback cycles in the system, and the system responds to these via other feedback cycles in a non-linear and scarcely predictable manner. Thus, in addition to the intended changes, there are also – always – unintended consequences if one attempts to overcome the limits set by scaling.

Increasing returns to scale in the Internet economy attract financial investors seeking extra profit. This leads to venture investments and drives financial bubbles, as seen recently with the *dot-com* bubble. New derivatives, originally intended to diversify risk, result in even more risky behaviour and eventually in financial crises of global scale. The public advertisement of the latest scientific results in social media, in line with over-simplification and over-selling, leads to a decrease in reputation not just of individual researchers, but of whole scientific disciplines.

A way out?

The only way of mitigating unintended consequences is to better understand the system by means of a systemic perspective. There are several limits to scaling which need to be *detected* and *respected*.

Bigger is not better: decreasing returns to scale render further growth unprofitable. And increasing returns to scale lead directly to bursting bubbles. Thus it makes no sense to just stretch the limits to growth, or to scaling.

Moreover, *small is not beautiful*: the occurrence of emergent phenomena beyond certain thresholds may lead to completely different systems and render our up-scaled knowledge from smaller systems useless. But *more is different*. And we need to understand in which way.

Frank Schweitzer has been professor for systems design at the Swiss Federal Institute of Technology ETH Zurich since 2004. His research focuses on applications of complex systems theory in the dynamics of social and economic organizations.

Haseeb Ahmed

Wind Tunnel World: Where the Wind Blows Straight

Haseeb Ahmed

Wind Tunnel World: Where the Wind Blows Straight

Dear CEO Steve Easterbrook and Esteemed
McDonald's Board of Directors,

It is with great pleasure that I write to you today on behalf of the experimental Wind Tunnel World community with a proposal which all may benefit from. As fellow producers of universal experiences, I invite you to consider the following proposal for a merger: both wind tunnels and McDouble cheeseburgers transcend time and place insofar as they reproduce an idiosyncratic sameness at any time and any place in the world. In this way they can be used to create a world beyond scale, time and geographic space. What we share is a belief in universality itself.

In your video statement earlier this year you state, "No business or brand has the divine right to succeed." A successfully totalized global society is made by people and for people. This is inevitably the principle of growth in capitalism. The question is what form shall it take? With 35,000 restaurants worldwide that serve roughly 68,000,000 people daily, McDonald's certainly produces a ubiquitous experience for the world to share through a single brand.

Your Big Mac is used as an international indicator of value;[1] however, after this year's fiscal report, you state that this project is in jeopardy.

The particular type of universality that exists within what I am calling the "Wind Tunnel World" (WTW) is lesser known to the general public of the world but is of no less ubiquity in their daily lives. All things that move through the air, or move air through them, must pass through the threshold of a wind tunnel before entering our industrially produced world. The list includes every car, airplane, bicycle helmet, HVAC system, windmill, skyscraper, city master plan, and much more. The wind and hunger are pre-existing conditions of the world that we are making adequate to our society. Within the WTW we have also found an ideal consumer for you.

Please allow me to share with you the brief history that is the firmament of the WTW followed by our preliminary studies for the merger, and its projected effects. This proposal may seem astounding but I believe you will find the argumentation entirely rational.

Origins of the Wind Tunnel World

Wind tunnels were not produced in order to jump between one place and another but rather to jump between the scale model and a full-scale product. However, the effort to make all wind tunnels equivalent to one another, so they could verify one another, has had the inadvertent effect of producing the Wind Tunnel World: the only place where the wind blows straight, while in Nature, the wind is endlessly turbulent. We can enter this Wind Tunnel World through any wind tunnel with laminar flow.

Wind tunnels have been erected throughout the world since the early 20th century and now compose a global network within which the WTW exists. The WTW was created as an inadvertent consequence of the attempt to systematically study cloud formations, weather patterns and vehicles for manned flight. In order to do this in accordance with scientific method, a controlled space had to

1 Online at http://www.economist.com/content/big-mac-index?fsrc=scn/fb/te/bl/ed/bigmacindex (accessed 26 September 2016).

be furnished in which phenomena could be isolated and studied. Natural phenomena, such as large global weather patterns outside, could thus be reproduced to scale inside of a wind tunnel.

Prior to their reproduction these phenomena were first experienced one to one in sailplanes. Upholding the traditions that founded aeronautical and atmospheric research, I took a trip to learn how to fly sailplanes with researchers at the von Karman Institute (VKI) for Fluid Dynamics, a NATO facility on the outskirts of Brussels. Originating in 1922, the VKI dates back to the founding years of the field. While flying over the historic Laucha Flugplatz in Eastern Germany[2] I learned that one of the two most important instruments on-board is the view of the horizon itself or *Horizontbild*, a mental geophysical picture that consists of a certain ratio of sky to earth. This ratio informs speed and position to a pilot while in the flux of flight. The second is a piece of yarn attached to the Plexiglas canopy of the cockpit. It should always appear as a straight line, up and down in relation to the body of the aircraft. This ensures that the plane is flying straight through the air and not slipping sideways through space.

Informed by this simple piece of yarn a global infrastructure would emerge. This straightness would be translated to what is now called laminar flow in wind tunnels. Laminar flow is a condition of wind moving in a straight line through the test section of a wind tunnel. This uniformity of the directionality of wind in wind tunnels exists nowhere in Nature and yet it allows for any natural condition to be reproduced within a wind tunnel. This is the paradoxical condition that has given birth to the Wind Tunnel World and its inhabitant, the ideal consumer of which I spoke earlier.

Scientific method and the age-old intense desire for manned flight called for the creation of this controlled space; however, it could not exist in isolation. In order for fact to be proven as fact, upon which technical innovation can proceed, it must be verifiable in any place at any time. Verification in experimental research means

2 Germany was banned from building motorized aircraft after each world war and is now the centre of the gliding world. Luftwaffe cadets trained in sailplanes before motorized ones were produced.

reproduction of experiments arriving at identical results insofar as lab procedure is followed. Each of these places, whether in Brazil or Belarus, no matter where or when, is in fact the same place While these places were made to test models of conditions and vehicles, some of these models became calibration objects in tests that aimed to ensure each wind tunnel could produce or reproduce the same results.

We believe that this consistency and the subsequent WTW that exists within it is the closest humanity has ever come to universality. However, we reach a dilemma of solipsistic proportions with this propagation. Are we describing the world outside of these conditions or creating a new one? Similarly, you may ask yourselves "Do people eat McDonald's because they like the food or because McDonald's is available anywhere at any time by being built into the infrastructure of motorized cities and in turn creating its own behavioural logic?"

The decision taken to use wind tunnels as the primary form of study of aero and environmental conditions was the resolution to invest in global infrastructure, as early whitepapers can attest to. National interests precipitated the arming of aircraft in the world wars, and each country began independently investing in this infrastructure instead. Starting in 1911, our predecessors in wind tunnel research, led by Sir Leonard Bairstow at the United Kingdom's National Physics Laboratory (NPL), began the endeavour to harmonize the wind tunnels of the world. Two objects were sent out to all of the First World War allies' wind tunnel facilities. After each test they were returned to the NPL in London and retested to ensure that the objects had not been altered. This process of ensuring the precision of the calibration objects meant that the test would take 11 years to conclude.

Tuning Forks of the Wind Tunnel World

What were these objects that tuned the world? The first was the RAF15 aerofoil profile, one of many standard wing designs. The second was a model of the R33 airship. The R33 airship had a previous life as the L33 zeppelin. The massive state-of-the-art airship had been shot down after an air raid over London in 1916. Its hydrogen exhausted, the German crew was unable to set it alight and it was captured by the British and reverse-engineered into R33.

Germany was not included in these international tests. Spreading a guarded German design to each of the Allied countries ensured the absence of the Germans from this endeavour. The national prejudices activated during the First World War had already permeated culture, including the seemingly objective sciences. Furthermore, the denial of Ludwig Prandtl's *Boundary Layer Theory* also ensured a fundamental flaw in these tests. The boundary layer theory concerns the area of mixing between straight-moving laminar flow and ambient free-stream flows that are especially important in quantifying the effect of the walls of wind tunnels on the flows they contain.

These early tests succeeded in standardizing aeronautic lab procedure and the researchers themselves rather than their labs. The 1928 "Report 309: Joint Report on Standardization Tests on N.P.L. R.A.F. 15 Airfoil Model" from the U.S. Navy's McCook Field compares results from McCook, Langley Field and M.I.T. and concludes: "The agreement between the results from various wind tunnels, obtained in comparative tests of this type depends almost entirely on the care used in making the tests." In 1923 Theodore von Kármán, a protégé of Prandtl's who joined the Allies, had already issued a statement together with other prominent wind-tunnel researchers of the time. He stated "it would be best to have the same model make a round trip to every laboratory adapted for such work" and that the "first step should be a preliminary conference between a few of the most prominent scientists and technical men… for creating an international scientific aeronautical association which is the best for bringing about a much desirable cooperation among aerodynamical research workers."[3]

You will agree that the standardization is incredibly important in your industry of fast food as well. You deliver the expected

3 Knight, William, Ludwig Prandtl, et al., 1923, *Standardization and Aerodynamics*. Washington D.C.: National Advisory Committee for Aeronautics.

same taste of a double cheeseburger whether eaten in 2008 and 2016 at location #2499 in Clinton, New York, or location #22009337 in Taqah, Oman. For you, the equivalent of laminar flow is a conditioned taste that is the idiosyncratic sum of its ingredients to which no other thing in the world tastes similar. The equivalent to the Wind Tunnel World may be the particular condition of desire and satisfaction beyond necessity of hunger regulated by the distinctive experience that can be had anywhere at any time, by patrons.

The development and use of this class of calibration objects has continued steadily for over 100 years until today. Given that each wind tunnel lab has been calibrated and tuned to one another using the present perfected calibration objects and techniques, all wind tunnels have equivalent conditions to the extent that when I step into a wind tunnel I may as well be stepping into any other. For instance, when I enter the Wright Brothers Wind Tunnel at the Massachusetts Institute of Technology I also enter its Second World War nemesis, the Adlershof wind tunnels outside of Berlin, or the Temple of Winds, the artistic wind tunnel in Zurich.[4] One can finally be in two or more places at once.

Topography of the Wind Tunnel World

The first wind tunnel calibration objects expressed the relationship of society to the air at the time. They were flying machines, a wing and a blimp, and if we look down from the altitude of their flight we can see that this Wind Tunnel World is substantial, that it even has topography.

So far this topography consists of three landmarks: two hills and a mountain. Askervein Hill was the first to be spotted; originally on an island in remote Northern Scotland, it was sighted in the WTW in 1997. Bolund Hill in Western Denmark came into view in the WTW in 2011. Most recently Alaiz Mountain, originally from Spain, was encountered in 2013. The topographies of these geographical features have been completely quantified. They have

4 The Temple of Winds is a Gottingen-type wind tunnel created by the 'Size Matters' research group at the Zurich University of the Arts in 2013 and continues to operate until present.

been taken up as prototypical representatives for potential wind farms to be built globally in light of the ecological crisis wrought by the use of fossil fuels. The thoroughness of the study of their surfaces allowed for the creation of models that were distributed throughout the world and used as calibration objects to further tune these wind tunnels so that they can participate in the collective study of wind energy. Wind energy is a contemporary concern of fluid dynamics beyond flying machines, which has also remained.

If you search for these geographic features with online mapping sites like Google Maps, the results do not take you to their location on the Earth's surface. Rather, one is consistently directed to one aeronautics research institute or another, public or private. While they are actual places, they exist more within the distributed but integral Wind Tunnel World than in the geographic one.

The WTW is derived from the world but not the same thing as it. It is selectively composed and in no apparent order aside from that of global capital, as identifiable locations in the WTW are near centres of capital. In the distance we can see a city arising, which is Oklahoma City in the western United States. In this case, the investment in a complete mapping of the wind and urban terrain of Oklahoma City and making that data public enabled it to proliferate as a calibration object for wind tunnels globally to the extent that it appeared in the Wind Tunnel World. Also on the horizon are nine perfect cubes that can be any urban centre. These cities are traversed by prototypical cars formed as the Ahmed (no relation) Bluff Body. These cities and vehicles begin to prepare the WTW for human habitation.

Vortex-Faced Being

Indeed, a native being has been conceived in the WTW. While wind tunnels normally incubate technologies for the future, including weaponry, in this case a being has been incubated within the collective boundary layers of wind tunnels. Ancient Greeks invented the theory of the wind egg in which the wind could fertilize certain animals and people just as it did plants. This theory was believed for 2000 years and used by theologians as proof of the virgin birth of Mary, mother of Jesus. The fertilized were considered to be strictly female, and so the wind must be male.

Vortex-Faced Being experiment

When placing a delta wing inside of a wind tunnel a remarkable thing can be seen: vortexes shedding off of the edges of the wing create a three-dimensional turbulence pattern. By projecting a two-dimensional laser plane through this pattern the wind is embodied in a form. It has two eyes and what appears to be a mouth. By altering the angle of attack of the delta wing the face reveals its facial expressions. Researcher Piero Bisello and myself have identified some of these faces in three separate sessions in Rhode-Saint-Genèse (VKI), Brussels, and Antwerp, Belgium.

If the being has a face then perhaps it can speak some language. In these sessions we tried to communicate with the face of the wind using a variety of languages in an attempt to train it to speak humanly. The sessions were composed of four different language types: computer-generated synthetic Latin vocabulary, the poem "Red-Haired Man" by Daniil Kharms in a non-linear fashion, an emoticon calibration script, and live typing in an attempt to make real-time contact. The responses to the exposure to these texts were sonified using an aero-acoustic set-up. This set-up consisted of a microphone placed inside a near-perfect streamlined egg form to record the wind that penetrated the egg, in line with the Greek theory.

Fellow researcher Piero Bisello noted: "While we realized that anthropomorphization could be a paranoid projection of a generic self onto things that otherwise go unnoticed, the face of the being persisted and seemingly smiled back from an otherwise menacing reality. This being consistently appeared before us in each session, and the being itself is born of consistency of the laminar condition of the wind blowing uniformly straight. Therefore in moving forward with these sessions we presume the being will be drawn to properties of consistency. Wind egg insemination is a reproduction for the beings inseminated, not for the wind. By producing high levels of consistency from heterogeneous sources we believe that the wind being will propagate through it."

That is the incentive that we offer you in our proposed merger: if you provide us with the consistency that permeates your foodstuffs then we will provide you with an ideal consumer for it; one that thrives upon consistency. Our motivation for doing so is to populate the Wind Tunnel World and, if possible, eventually the world, with a non-corporeal being composed of wind. Furthermore, new forms of interaction and consummation between your 68 million customers and these beings could drastically increase the number of patrons frequenting both McDonald's and the WTW. While born of standardization, these interactions would be novel and warrant further patronage to your existing 35,000 locations, joined in number by the hundreds of operational wind tunnels worldwide. If the initial Greek wind egg theories prove to hold true, this could lead to the possibility of human reproduction without men and with the wind.

A note on isolated atmospheric particularity

The Vortex-Faced Being is able to reside within the particular isolation of the atmosphere of the WTW. Fluid dynamics, the larger discipline in which aeronautics now resides, relies on equations like the Navier-Stokes equations to mediate between one scale and another. The realities produced inside of wind tunnels are to scale. However, this scaling is not linear. The density of air remains fixed in most cases but is experienced differently at different sizes and different speeds. For instance, a house fly flies by creating a cushion of air upon which it rides through space while a jet plane creates a pressure differential over and under its wings to create lift. This means that not all of the reality of a chosen condition transcends into a wind tunnel for observation nor all of what is produced in a wind tunnel transcends back to the outside world. This insulation allows the Wind Tunnel World to exist parallel to our own.

Initial McDouble cheeseburger selection study

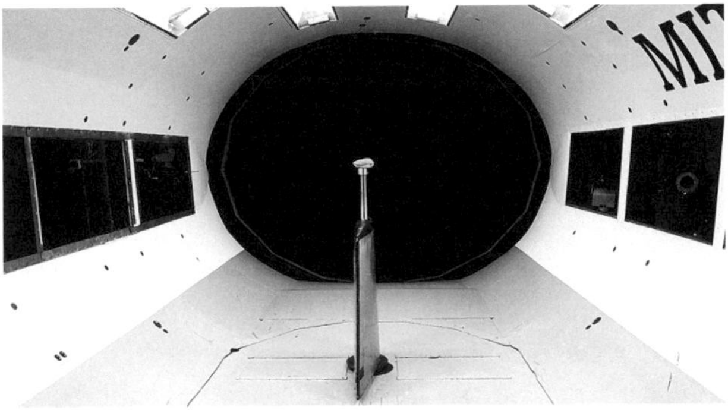

Fig. 5: HA 16. McDouble Wind Tunnel Calibration Test (Photo: Haseeb Ahmed at MIT Wright Brothers Wind Tunnel, Cambridge, MA, USA, 23 October 2015)

In Brussels on 27 August 2014 I ate the same hamburger as my brother did in Toledo, Ohio, at the same time. He ate his at the same McDonald's where I had eaten one in 1992 prior to his birth. This uniformity of experience over wide geographic spaces connecting different experiences of time makes it hard to know where we entered *sameness* or when it began. The experience of eating this object transcends both time and space. Consumers are freed from the limits of geographic space because time is collapsed into it.[5] The McDouble cheeseburger is one of the few remaining

5 This was written in 1923 in the aftermath of the 1917 Russian Revolution. Under Capitalism, "... [T]ime sheds its qualitative, variable, flowing nature; it freezes into an exactly delimited, quantifiable continuum filled with quantifiable 'things' (the reified, mechanically objectified 'performance' of the worker, wholly separated from his total human personality): in short, it becomes space. In this environment where time is transformed into abstract, exactly measurable, physical space, an environment at once the cause and effect of the scientifically and mechanically fragmented and specialised production of the object of labour, the subjects of labour must likewise be rationally fragmented. On the one hand, the objectification of their labour-power into something opposed to their total personality (a process already accomplished with the sale of that labour-power as a commodity) is now made into the permanent ineluctable reality of their daily life. Here, too, the personality can do no more than look on helplessly while its own existence is reduced to an isolated particle and fed into an alien system. On the other hand, the mechanical disintegration of the process of production into its components also destroys those bonds that had bound individuals to a community in the days when production was still 'organic'. In this respect, too, mechanisation makes of them isolated abstract atoms whose work no longer brings them together directly and organically; it becomes mediated to an increasing extent exclusively by the abstract laws of the mechanism which imprisons them" (Lukacs, Georg, 1971, *History and Class Consciousness: Studies in Marxist Dialectics*. Cambridge, MA: MIT Press: 90).

commodities in which Fordist economic vision still holds true, as the labourer at McDonald's may also be its consumer even though minimum wage has not increased with the cost of living in most US cities.

This capacity of the McDouble cheeseburger as standard object brought me to consider it as a calibration object for my experience of time over space. I am not alone in this socially generated reality. To further the advancement of the WTW it is necessary to create a new calibration object. The unique quality of the McDouble cheeseburger as a calibration object is that it can be consumed, thus allowing for a one-to-one experience of the body to the entire territory of the Wind Tunnel World. The previous calibration objects either moved through space or occupied it at much larger scales.

Wind tunnel McDouble experiment

To establish the McDouble as a standard wind-tunnel calibration object like those employed over the last 100 years, it was necessary to reproduce a study in multiple laboratories in different locations. Our primary method of measurement is flow visualization using smoke and a laser sheet to document the fleeting figuration of turbulence patterns with cameras.

The first test was carried out at the VKI's L7 Eiffel-type wind tunnel in Brussels on Friday, 2 October 2015. This is the same wind tunnel in which the Vortex-Faced Being was first seen. An incense stick generated the smoke and the laser sheet was created by means of a red diode laser with beam splitter. On Friday, 23 October 2015 a second test was conducted at the MIT Wright Brothers Wind Tunnel in Cambridge, Massachusetts, where the first R33 and RAF 15 calibration tests had also taken place. Lastly, on Friday, 4 December 2015 a test was conducted at the Temple of the Winds, the artistic wind tunnel of the 'Size Matters' research group at the Zurich University of the Arts.

Each of these tests showed that the same vortex pattern was being created by the McDouble cheeseburger. The vortex pattern is unique to the McDouble cheeseburger even though each of the cheeseburgers had been sourced from different locations nearest to the employed wind tunnel facilities. While unique, McDouble cheeseburgers are the same. This may have to do with the ubiquitous make-up as each of the two burger patties in the McDouble can contain beef from up to 100 cattle;[6] such is the equality we seek to propagate. The results of these verified experiments are promising and indicate a way in which the WTW could gain a larger portion of reality when consistently and diligently co-created by you, McDonald's.

The same degree of homogeneity exists in each of our respective products of food and vehicles, the results of which are distributed globally through vast infrastructures. However, our homogeneities are heterogeneous. Homogeneity in so far as it contains the kernel of universal experience for Homo sapiens. To make good on this potential rather than leave it to decay in isolated realms or bring it into destructive contest, we now propose to you: let's homogenize our two different homogeneities towards a homogeneity of a greater universal capacity than either of us can achieve alone. We suggest the slogan "Homo Homo Homo!" for any promotional material that may be deployed in the future. As stated above, we believe that this merger is one of man and wind and this will yield a new form of subjectivity beyond the strictly terrestrial. This new form of subjectivity will have new consumer desires for you to meet, opening up entirely new markets.

In aeronautics we are bound to develop technology for those with the greatest amount of capital, which are military contractors and industrial transport. Subsequently, the supernatural conditions existing in our wind tunnels increasingly deliver expertise. Similarly, the transcendence achieved by McDonald's is limited to the modest form of burgers and fries. Tragically this hard-fought universality of human experience could be lost to banality and made impotent, even fattening before its potential can be realized. The merger would allow for moving beyond the constraints that bind us. We know that your true aim is more than the production of

6 Online at www.mcdonalds.co.uk/ukhome/whatmakesmcdonalds/questions/food/beef/do-mcdonalds-burgers-contain-beef-from-up-to-100-or-or-even-1000-different-cows.html (accessed 26 September 2016).

foodstuffs, just as ours is not to produce only automobiles, windmills and airplanes. Rather, your aim is to create universalized social experience, and 68 million people daily can attest to it. On our side, 220 million Americans alone drive cars and 8 million people worldwide fly each day. In doing so, each person experiences the conditions of the WTW by which their vehicles for travel were formed.

Conclusions and future prospects

In our field we saw the movement of a piece of yarn yield an entire reality of the Wind Tunnel World that had never existed before. In you, McDonald's, we see the creation of a shared global reality. Like the wind tunnel calibration objects of Askervein and Bolund hill, which exist in both the WTW and the dominant reality at once, we see the McDouble's promise. The integration of our two realities will create another world where the same conditions will exist consistently throughout – a laminar world that is truly in and of itself.

With your support we will conduct the McDouble tuning experiment in additional wind tunnels throughout the world, and the same unique vortex pattern will appear shedding from the McDouble. Up until now we have had cities, geographic features, and flying machines produced to scale as models for wind tunnels. With the 1:1 McDouble we reverse this flow. Instead of reproducing the outside world inside of wind tunnels at a smaller scale to create a universal condition, we will be able to take the universal condition that now exists inside of wind tunnels and reproduce it at a larger scale outside of them. At the apex of this decisive moment the Vortex-Faced Being has appeared to consummate the scales as an ideal consumer of this ideal object of the McDouble cheeseburger to join the millions who have already experienced this universality. The universal condition is transferred and united.

While the former experiments entailed total mapping of research sites and remodelling of them, complex equations to mitigate the consequences of scale effects, and drawn-out logistics to check the integrity of the individual calibration objects, McDouble cheeseburgers are available worldwide. When combined with the world-wide network of wind tunnels we may be able to deliver the first, fastest and cheapest utopia.

Industry concretises and proliferates according to its own massive standards of production; however, this approach can render this fragile universality as banality safe for consumption if we are not careful. This universality of human experience is a miracle of science but spoken about by the general public in terms of excess fat, in your case, or as a nerds' domain, in ours. The potential is lost on most, but this condition we propose to create together engenders not only scientific universality but also social equality, which capitalism brings forth and in the same moment withholds. For instance, while the hour is a universalized unit of measure, the value of a labour hour differs greatly between one place and another. This is why we are writing you today, our colleagues who command the world's largest food producers to have ever existed. We are convinced that you fully understand the possibilities standardization can deliver. The bonding of mankind through the particular experience of movement and the particular gaining of nutrients is grounded in scientific reason. All may profit, not just the interested communities. When I refer to all, I mean the global population that both our fields serve.

Sincerely,

Haseeb Ahmed,
Wind Tunnel World Ambassador

Haseeb Ahmed (*1985, Toledo, Ohio, USA) is a research-based artist who often works collaboratively to integrate tools and techniques from the hard sciences in order to produce artworks. His project with wind tunnels is a PhD in practice-based arts with the University of Antwerp, Zurich University of the Arts, von Karman Institute and Sint Lucas Antwerp University College of Art and Design. Ahmed is represented by Harlan Levey Projects.

Olivier Chazot

Scaling! What Scaling? A Note on Fluid Dynamics Experiments and Research Experience

Olivier Chazot

Scaling! What Scaling? A Note on Fluid Dynamics Experiments and Research Experience

Science investigates Nature and looks at it in the light of its own questions. Its evolution follows conceptual and theoretical developments which open up fields of research that are explored in all directions. It also sometimes comes up against strong barriers brought by new findings that make it necessary to reconsider its fundamentals. In such cases, these investigations are accompanied by experiments that aim to observe, measure and amass knowledge of natural phenomena. Nature is what it is, and science remains a general perspective on the things that can capture all the details for their accurate description, serving as a reliable map. However, science always stays distant from the essential ground it intends to represent. Moreover, if it seeks to grasp the object of study in itself it loses the knowledge it aims to gather. All of this depends on whether science is able to figure out the workings of Nature and manages to achieve a robust reproduction of phenomena through experiments and computations.

Scientists developed the language of Nature from the 17th century onwards with the rise of positive science. Mathematics stood out as a very fruitful and efficient path to this aim. This framework still opens doors for a variety of developments. In particular, it provides the tools needed to design the conditions of reproduction of natural phenomena in the controlled environment of a laboratory. This paves the way for the experimental approach that appears as a more direct channel to reality inasmuch as it brings physics to the laboratory level. One succeeds in this operation thanks to the theoretical description of Nature that makes it possible to scale physical phenomena.

This view does not apply equally in all fields of natural science. Some of these fields remain largely empirical and wait for concepts to emerge for a theoretical description. This is the case, for example, in the life sciences where even though tremendous progress has been made in genetics and molecular biology, the reductionist approach remains very difficult because one needs to account for the numerous parameters that interact in living processes. However the reductionist approach is highly suitable for a classical discipline like mechanics, which is at the root of modern science and is "one of the branches of physics in which the number of principles is at once very few and very rich in useful consequences" (Dugas 1950). Specifically, in the discipline of fluid dynamics conservation equations apply and the role of experiment is essential. Experimentation is essential firstly because it offers direct contact with Nature – in this case the physics of flow – going beyond speculative science. Secondly, it is also essential because experiments are one of only two possible ways of finding solutions to fluid dynamic equations that rule flows.

The application of thermodynamics and Newton's Laws to describe the dynamics of a fluid has a long history in mechanics. They converged to establish the Navier-Stokes equations in the mid-19th century. They are a set of equations that express the conservation of mass, momentum and energy for a volume of fluid. Those equations correspond to the modelling of a flow. It presents numerous properties and non-linear terms in particular. This last feature impedes, in most cases, analytical integration. Thus engineers are able to write mathematical models of flows but then are left with an equation they cannot solve. Nevertheless those equations can be written in a non-dimensional form where characteristic numbers appear as coefficients of the terms of the equation and represent their relative importance (fig. 1).

$$\mathrm{St}\cdot\frac{\partial v^*}{\partial t^*}+v^*.\nabla v^*=-\mathrm{Eu}\cdot\nabla p^*+\frac{1}{\mathrm{Re}}\nabla^2 v^*+\frac{1}{\mathrm{Fr}}\cdot f$$

Strouhal Euler Reynolds Froude

$x^*=x/L$ $y^*=y/L$ $z^*=z/L$ $v^*=v/U$ $t^*=t/(L/U)$

Fig. 1: Navier-Stokes equation in dimensionless form (momentum balance)

These dimensionless numbers (as mentioned in fig. 1 *St, Eu, Re, Fr*) express the ratio of two physical phenomena present in a flow. They are denominated by the names of the scientists that study their influence or formulate their expression. The Reynolds number is the most important dimensionless group in fluid mechanics. Almost all viscous-flow phenomena depend upon the Reynolds number (White 2006: 82). It represents the ratio of the forces of inertia to the viscous forces in the flow (fig. 2).

$$\mathrm{Re} = \frac{\rho.U.L}{\mu}$$

U: velocity
L: length
ρ: density
μ: Viscosity

Fig. 2: Reynolds number expression

Thanks to its non-dimensional formulation, this fluid dynamics equation can be written for a flow in a laboratory situation just as it can be written for a full-scale environment for a real-flow application. As long as the dimensionless numbers are the same, the two flows, even at completely different scales, are equivalent and the solution is the same. Finally, one could reproduce in a lab the flow phenomena that evolved at a much larger or sometimes much smaller scale (fig. 3). To preserve the Reynolds number *Re*, similarly, the reduced length *L*, for example, could be compensated by higher velocity *U* and higher density ρ. Thus $Re = (\rho_1 \cdot U_1 L_1)/\mu = (\rho_2 \cdot U_2 L_2)/\mu$, in this case $L_1 > L_2$, but $\rho_1 < \rho_2$ and $U_1 < U_2$. Indeed some physical limits should be considered and the velocity U_2 must not be too high to prevent the compressible effects to appear at lower scale.

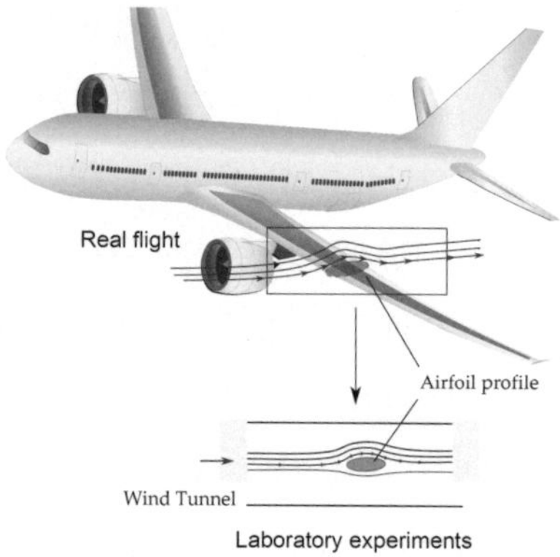

Fig. 3: Correspondence between real flight and simulated flight in wind tunnel testing of a scaled aerofoil

The scaling process is intimately linked to the mathematization of Nature that is expressed in the modelling of a flow. The governing equations for a fluid motion can be written without dimension. They then can be adapted to any scales and apply to real applications as they do in the lab environment. Hence the outside phenomena can be isolated and reproduced to any scale inside a controlled lab setting with fidelity.

On the ground, engineers have developed wind tunnels. These are facilities that allow for the recreation of flow conditions at smaller scale while respecting the characteristic dimensionless numbers derived from the Navier-Stokes equation. A typical wind tunnel is represented in figure 4. The flow condition of interest is reproduced in the test section where flow phenomena can be observed and measured around a scaled model. The settling chamber and the contraction placed upstream and the diffuser connected downstream guarantee optimum flow quality and suitable conditions at the position of the model. The model is often a small-scale reproduction of a vehicle or large structure that interacts with the wind or moves through the air. It is the interaction between the model and the flow condition that recreates the large-scale realities of interest to engineers.

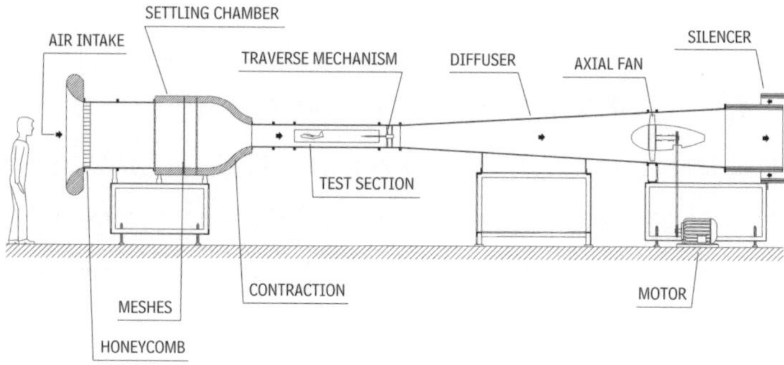

Fig. 4: VKI L-2A Wind tunnel for low speed testing

From this perspective, Nature is viewed as a mechanical system that could be expressed with a mathematical formulation. The streamlines of a flow that pass around a model in a test section of a wind tunnel are indeed physical lines. Flow visualization techniques can make these lines visible to the naked eye through the introduction of smoke and other substrates as well as controlled light. However, these lines also can be interpreted as mathematical functions that are solutions of the equations that have been written to describe the dynamics of the flow. Wind tunnels therefore enable engineers to solve the Navier-Stokes equations. The principle of scaling in fluid mechanics is a natural result of this conception. The flow is a continuum and a direct bijection can be defined between the fluid phenomena from the full scale in a natural environment to the flow in wind tunnel experiments, on scaled models (mock-ups), in the laboratory. This connection results directly from the mathematical modelling of a flow. The flow model in this case is a set of equations that can be written without dimension and adapted to any scale.

For fluid mechanics, scaling is not a particular issue. Science has no ambitions to ask, "Why is scaling possible?" Rather, science proposes ways in which scaling is possible. However, if one examines the importance of experiments in science, and considers wind tunnels in particular, one is brought back automatically to the question of scaling. An experiment in fluid dynamics represents a problem in general; it gives a solution for a family of flows, for whatever flows correspond to the model mechanical science has defined. However, our knowledge of the world is based on our models that incarnate it. This is the way we question the world and how we want to see it, a way that results directly from how we represent Nature. Nevertheless, because an experiment happens at a particular scale and in a particular environment that brings Nature to the level of our reference, Nature comes to our perception and forms an experience for which the world no longer serves as the first reality or evidence, but where it rather becomes a question in itself.

Scientific experiments bring the world to our level. Scaling used in experiments to bring phenomena to the human reference is not a projection that is above or below reality, as explained by Maurice Merleau-Ponty (1964: 275). It is the real at the disposal of our perception (fig. 5).

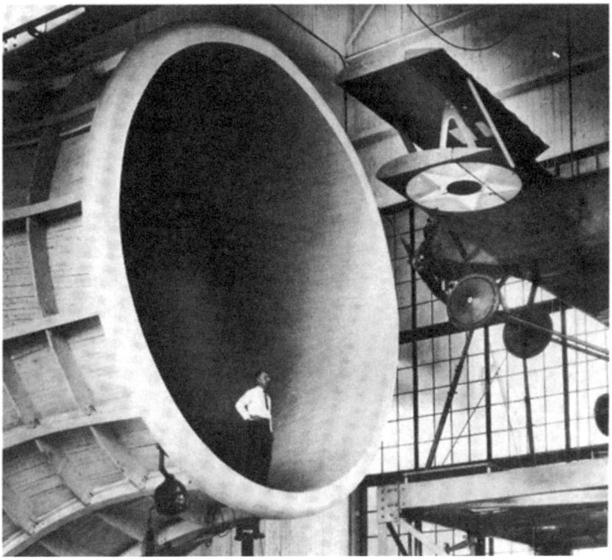

Fig. 5: Knowledge is the place where we meet the world (Picture: Baals and Corliss 1981)

Experiments, as presented earlier, are derived from a rational framework. They are set up to develop and produce knowledge from the solutions they allow us to access. Scaling has an important role in the experimental process. It is the consequence of the mathematical description of a flow, but also brings us closer to its nature. Knowledge is the place where we meet the world. Nevertheless knowledge always lags behind understanding. As

Hannah Arendt wrote: "Understanding precedes and succeeds knowledge. Preliminary understanding, which is at the basis of all knowledge, and true understanding, which transcends it, have this in common: they make knowledge meaningful" (2015: 311).

Scaling is manifested in experiments that result from a representation of the world; however experiments are also an experience of the world accessible to our perception. Science goes uniformly from the big scale to the smaller one as long as the same model can be applied. It is a common cliché to associate Sir Isaac Newton's vision of the Moon with an apple, both of which obey the laws of gravity at different scales. Each level of scaling is able to provide a portion of reality and capture aspects of physics in infinite details. However, science remains a general vision that generates knowledge that in turn fails to penetrate the essence of Nature.

Where science stops, experiments continue. When science proceeds with its investigations and questions and balks at difficulties to capture physics, experiments are not bounded since experiments initially derived from a scientific approach are not limited to the scientific results they produce. Their influence extends to the experience through which we receive the world. With scaling, experiments reach human reference and hence experience, they become a performance to access the presence of Nature.

References

Arendt, Hannah, 2015, *Essays in Understanding: 1930–1954*. New York: Schocken Books.

Baals, Donald D., and William R. Corliss, 1981, *Wind Tunnels of NASA*, NASA SP-440. Washington DC: National Aeronautics and Space Administration. Online at http://history.nasa.gov/SP-440/cover.htm (accessed 26 September 2016).

Dugas, René, 1950, *Histoire de la mécanique*. Paris: Editions Dunod.

White, Frank M., 2006, *Viscous Fluid Flow*, 3rd Edition. New York: McGraw-Hill International Edition.

Merleau-Ponty, Maurice, 1964, *Le visible et l'invisible (Bibliothèque des idées)*. Paris: Gallimard.

Olivier Chazot (*1970, Lyon) is an aerospace researcher who studies aerothermodynamics phenomena in planetary re-entries, from ground testing facilities to real flight missions. He is the head of the Aeronautics and Aerospace Department at the Von Karman Institute and teaches hypersonic gas dynamics.